# THE
# CHARACTER
# TRIANGLE

# LORNE RUBIS

"Lorne Rubis' *The Character Triangle* enables you to write your own playbook to effectively and constructively 'play' in the game of life! A concise, to the point, and practical guide. Superb!"
— Gary Ames, retired CEO, MediaOne International

"*The Character Triangle* is a virtual GPS to successful relationship management — both personal and business. Inspirational, highly relevant and full of insights and advice from a talented leader ... an exceptionally valuable tool for managers."
— Larry Berg, President and CEO,
Vancouver International Airport Authority

"*The Character Triangle* is a testament to Lorne Rubis' deep understanding of the links between performance and humanity. Rubis has a way of extracting simplicity from complex 'real life' experiences. His stories are compelling and heartfelt — sometimes he wins, sometimes he loses — but each experience leads to a profound lesson the reader can apply to everyday life. If you follow the guidance in this book, you will be a stronger, more productive, and more fulfilled human being. Lorne Rubis is fast becoming one of life's great teachers. Read the book!"
— Jamie Brunner, Founder and CEO, Kinetix Living Inc.

"*The Character Triangle* is a wonderful read and an important book for anyone interested in living a values-filled life filled with abundance and inspiration. With a helpful framework for decision making, informed by a lifetime of real-world experience, Lorne Rubis has written a thoughtful, interesting and ultimately helpful book for developing the character of your life and others."
— Daniel Debow, co-CEO, Rypple

"Lorne's advice is what is required in corporate America today. By reading and incorporating the suggestions of *The Character Triangle*, today's managers will undoubtedly become leaders with the ability to inspire their troops. Read it, believe it, and do it."
— Mike Delisle, CEO, International Certification Services, Inc.

"What a great read. Lorne speaks from experience in *The Character Triangle*. He's impacted and inspired thousands, directly and indirectly — myself included. This book provides the tools necessary for you to begin making changes on the inside — which ultimately shine through on the outside. The fact that Lorne practices what he preaches allows him to communicate the vision in a way that makes the difference."
— Bill Garcia, Co-founder and Managing Partner,
TableForce, Ltd.

"Lorne Rubis has taken three seemingly simple words and has added weight and substance to create a magnificent framework for leading in today's world. A must read for anyone serious about making an impact."
— Ross Gilchrist, Leader, Strategic Design and Talent,
Co-founder, The Next Institute Inc.

"In *The Character Triangle*, Lorne Rubis gives the reader both a "lens" with which to see him/herself in a new way and a "window" into the soul of a man who has lived the life of Accountability, Respect, and Abundance that he describes. I have known Lorne as a close friend for over twenty years. I have had the chance to observe him as a father, husband, and executive. In each of these roles, he is the same man — optimistic, compassionate, insightful, and curious. And his highly successful marriage and wonderful children are proof positive that Lorne's philosophy works at every level. I highly recommend his book. It will change your life."
— Greg Goodwin, CEO, Kuni Automotive

"I have known Lorne to be an authentic and a passionate people leader with great insights into human behavior in the workplace. This book is instructive and provides easy steps to building a strong personal character for lasting happiness."
— Firoz Lalji, CEO and Chairman, Zones, Inc.

"Lorne Rubis is a special leader. I knew it from the first time I met him as CEO of Ryzex. Over several years he has shared important lessons and stories from his life and his career that I have enjoyed and reflected on. I leave every encounter with Lorne smiling and thinking deeply. *The Character Triangle* captures his best. Time reading this book and performing the exercises is well invested."
— Derek Long, Executive Director, Sustainable Connections

"The news is rife with examples of corruption and deceit in corporations; frequently, at the core of those issues are the character traits of the leadership in those organizations... with that backdrop comes a book that is both timely and well written by an author whose experience is not academic but in the living and breathing world that is corporate America... In *The Character Triangle*, Lorne Rubis shares more than just a framework for leading; he shares his story, his life, and, at the center, the character traits that have been his guideposts. I have known Lorne for a long time... as a boss, as a colleague, and as a friend... in all these years, the traits Lorne writes about are ones that he not only lived by but, more importantly, demanded his team learn, live, and teach."
— David R. McCauley, Consultant; former COO Barking Software and VP Sales, Micron Electronics

"Great leaders come in all shapes and sizes with a wide range of experiences, knowledge, and abilities. What they all have in common, however, is great character. In the *The Character Triangle*, Lorne Rubis provides a terrific framework to be applied by all who desire to lead and lead well."

— Dick McCormick, Chairman Emeritus, US WEST

"I encourage the reader to listen to what Lorne has to say with a serious intent, because what he offers is not only wise but is also a practical playbook for personal and professional success. I have known Lorne for over 30 years as a friend and business colleague. I know that Lorne speaks from experience and "walks the talk." He has developed and incorporated *The Character Triangle* in his daily life and along with hard work and determination has achieved enviable personal and professional success. Now, with his abundance, he shares his ideas that helped him grow a loving family and become a respected and impactful Chief Executive."

— Thomas W. McDade, Jr., PhD,
Co-founder, Deltapoint Consulting

"I have worked alongside of Lorne Rubis in a difficult turnaround technology company that tested, demonstrated, and proved that his playbook outlined in *The Character Triangle* works and can form a basis for personal and business success in any situation. I applaud him for writing this book and sharing his insights."

— Kirby McDonald, Chairman and CEO, Pioneer Ventures

"This book is remarkable for a number of reasons, first and perhaps foremost because of its author, who in my experience has been a living embodiment of the three simple principles that make up the character triangle. Second, because of its simplicity, the concept is not hard to understand — the challenge lies in the personal commitment required to live the promise you make to yourself as a leader every single day... or should. Third, because it's about you, and me, and about the way in which we choose to lead our lives, and impact the people around us. Management is a title, but leadership is a choice — one every single individual has the power to make every single day — and this book helps make that choice the only one any true leader, or aspiring leader, can make. As Lorne says, live the triangle."

— Gopal RajGuru, Partner, Infoteam Consulting

"*The Character Triangle* has the power to transform you as a person and a leader. I have experienced the privilege of working with and for Lorne in an environment where under his leadership *The Character Triangle* powerfully transformed my life and the culture around us. If you are in a role of influencing the thoughts, actions and behaviors of others, you are a leader. Understanding these specific character attributes and having the practical tools to help live them are essential to personal success in all aspects of being a leader in life!"

— Todd Rawls, former COO and CFO, Ryzex Inc., and Executive Pastor, North County Christ the King

"Having had the first hand opportunity to hire for a small company, work with in a large company, and work for Mr. Rubis in a start up I whole heartedly concur with his lifelong observations of people, work, and family. You too will 'stand up and applaud' at home and at work if you choose to apply the practical, thoughtful and concise opportunity presented through the personal application of principles *The Character Triangle*."

— John Scully, rancher, lawyer, Montana scallywag, and former Vice President Public Policy, US WEST

"A truly remarkable business leader and human being, Lorne Rubis lives everything he advises us about in his inspiring book of insights, *The Character Triangle: Build Character, Have an Impact and Inspire Others*. Summarizing a lifetime of his 'best practices' in developing outstanding character and leadership qualities, Rubis highlights essential knowledge and thinking skills everyone needs for managing one's personal and professional relationships with common sense and compassion. Lorne offers priceless practical wisdom for self-learning and exercising those healthy habits of mind that enable us all to be creative, trustworthy, respected and kindhearted leaders: individuals with abundant abilities who empower others to lead and thrive, as well."

— Todd Siler, PhD, author of *Think Like A Genius*

# THE
# CHARACTER TRIANGLE

BUILD CHARACTER,
HAVE *an* IMPACT,
*and* INSPIRE OTHERS

# LORNE RUBIS

Langdon Street Press
Minneapolis, MN

Langdon Street Press
212 3ʳᵈ Avenue North, Suite 290
Minneapolis, MN 55401
612.455.2293
www.langdonstreetpress.com

The author gratefully acknowledges permission to reprint the poem
"Kindness" by Naomi Shihab Nye.

ISBN-13: 978-1-936782-60-4
LCCN: 2011938740

Distributed by Itasca Books

Typeset by Melanie Shellito
Character Triangle illustrations are by Alese Pickering.

*Printed in the United States of America*

# DEDICATION

*For Kathleen, my generous and loving wife who has been*
*at my side since high school, and our remarkable children:*
*Keely, Jillian, and Garrett, my inspiration for self-discovery*
*and developing the Character Triangle.*

*For my parents,*
*Leo and Mary; they are the foundation and example*
*of all that defines character.*

# CONTENTS

Foreword by Chuck Lillis . . . . . . . . . . . . . . . . . . . . . . . . . . xv

Foreword by Rud Browne . . . . . . . . . . . . . . . . . . . . . . . . . xvii

Chapter 1—Introduction . . . . . . . . . . . . . . . . . . . . . . . . . . . 1

Chapter 2—BE Accountable . . . . . . . . . . . . . . . . . . . . . . . 13

*"Why is This Happening to ME?"*
*Why the Blame Game Never Works*
*Key Steps to Becoming More Accountable*
*Do You Know Someone Like Sam?*
*Do You Know Someone Like Jim?*
*So Much of How We Choose to Act is*
*Under Our Personal Control*
*The Be Accountable Playbook*
*Practice the Plays*
*Personal Learning on Being Accountable*

Chapter 3—BE Respectful . . . . . . . . . . . . . . . . . . . . . . . . 49

*(Self) Respect Starts Within*
*So Respect is to be Earned, Right?*
*Everything is a Process*
*Listen with Understanding*
*Embrace Diversity*
*Be Nice, Be Kind*
*Be Present*
*Do You Know Someone Like Juanita?*

*Do You Know Someone Like Geraldo?*
*The BE Respectful Playbook*
*Practice the Plays*
*Personal Learning on Being Respectful*

Chapter 4—BE Abundant . . . . . . . . . . . . . . . . . . . . . . . . . . . 85

*It's All About the Attitude: Abundance Versus Scarcity*
*Abundance as a State of Mind*
*Do You Know Someone Like Fatimah?*
*Do You Know Someone Like Raj?*
*The BE Abundant Playbook*
*Practice the Plays*
*Personal Learning on Being Abundant*

Chapter 5—Character Triangle Points to Remember . . . . 119

*Be Accountable, Be Respectful and Be Abundant:*
*A Connected System*
*Everything is a Process — the Process is Everything*
*We Define Success*
*Connect your Purpose to the Character Triangle*
*"Kindness" a poem by Naomi Shihab Nye*

Appendix A: What and How. . . . . . . . . . . . . . . . . . . . . . . . 135

Appendix B: Situation—Target—Proposal . . . . . . . . . . . . . 137

Acknowledgments. . . . . . . . . . . . . . . . . . . . . . . . . . . . . . . . 141

About the Author. . . . . . . . . . . . . . . . . . . . . . . . . . . . . . . . . 143

Bibliography and References. . . . . . . . . . . . . . . . . . . . . . . . 145

Index . . . . . . . . . . . . . . . . . . . . . . . . . . . . . . . . . . . . . . . . . . . 151

# FOREWORD

The challenges facing leaders, and the attributes foundational to their success, are many and complex. We see and understand the true value of outstanding leadership when the situation is most critical, complicated, and broadly impactful. These "situations" occur in the public arena, within families, and in businesses. Many of us are leaders in multiple environments and most of us, I suspect, spend time each day auditing our personal leadership abilities, actions, and methods. Often, we are our own harshest critics!

*The Character Triangle* is, at a minimum, a wonderful articulation and user-friendly compilation of the most basic tenants of truly superior leadership. It is a "playbook" of sorts—a reminder of how personal belief systems interact with personal style to produce leadership qualities. Its pragmatic focus on what we believe and what we do is almost appropriate as a bedside nightly reader for the inspired leader. Rubis' "Triangle" of self-accountability, respect, and a belief in abundance rather than scarcity is as powerful in its simplicity as its interdependence. Rubis' explanation (and exploration) of each of these three factors and their relationships is wonderful reading.

But this is much more than a feel-good book about how great leadership should work. He cites numerous examples where great leadership relies on positive and humanitarian dispositions, but is not held captive to a naïve blindness to evil and misplaced ambition or practice. The great leader accepts and manages in all environments by recognizing the benefits of adherence to the Triangle attributes.

From both content and style perspectives, *The Character Triangle* will be valuable to leaders of all sorts, but perhaps most to entrepreneurs who have such a terrific opportunity to define their environment. The author's work is original— the product of an eclectic set of work and life experiences combined with a solid education. But he also does a terrific job of pulling together leadership learnings from dozens of students of the subject. The work of Rifkin, Peters, Friedman, Tolle, and others flows together with his own.

I love the challenge addressed to the reader. Know your purpose, your plan, and your values. Make leading a positive experience for those you lead. Rely on the Triangle. Simply put, as you drive for organizational accomplishment, remember that your colleague's dreams, ambitions, and hopes are just as important to them as yours are to you.

— Chuck Lillis, Founding Partner, Castle Pines Capital
Former Chairman and CEO, MediaOneGroup, Inc.

# FOREWORD

I have had the good fortune to watch Lorne passionately apply the principles of the Character Triangle and see the positive impact they have had on our team. They proved to be of particular value during the challenges we faced during the recent "Great Recession." Like most companies we were forced to make tough choices and ask our people to share the sacrifices.

This was made all the more difficult because, at the same time as the recession was upon us, an unprecedented number of unrelated personal challenges seemed to come out of nowhere, hitting many of our team members in other parts of their lives. Some days it seemed like everything that could go wrong, did!

We did however manage to weather the storms and have emerged as a stronger, better organization because of them. I believe that this was in large part because of the very values of Accountability, Abundance, and Respect that Lorne speaks to in this book and has promoted within our organization for years before the crisis.

**Accountability** served to remind all of us to focus on what our individual responsibilities and areas of influence were, while helping free us from the feelings of powerlessness that comes from fixating on what "others should be doing."

**Abundance** proved to be very helpful to me personally in one of my darkest moments. I had just finished a particularly difficult week and was preoccupied with what was "lacking" in my life. I applied the principle of Abundance to flip this around and remind myself of all the things I should be grateful for. I finished feeling truly humbled by my good fortune and wanted to remind myself of this every day. One simple way I found to do this is to end all my correspondence with the word "thanks" unless I feel it may be inappropriate or too informal in the circumstances to do so.

**Respect** was perhaps the most critical component during the crisis. Almost everyone within our organization was able to recognize that everybody else was feeling stressed and on edge during this period. Looking back, it's surprising how few people raised their voices or became disrespectful (even if they were being terminated). I believe respect resulted in us coming through this ordeal feeling closer and more trusting with each other as a result.

Like many organizations these values have been viewed as important to Ryzex, but also like many organizations, our approach to reinforcing them had been largely unconscious and haphazard. All of us have limits on our direct sphere of influence. One of the key challenges all entrepreneurs face is how to find ways to institutionalize the core values they know are necessary for lasting success.

Lorne's stories and techniques offer leaders a way to consciously reinforce these values within their organizations. I am sure you will enjoy and appreciate, as we have, Lorne's passion for finding ways to make Accountability, Abundance, and Respect a more conscious part of one's personal value system and organizational culture.

*Thanks,*

Rud Browne, Founder and Chairman, The Ryzex Group

# CHAPTER 1
## Introduction

The junior high school gym was stuffed with a few hundred hormone-infused kids between eleven and fourteen years of age. The year was 1975 and I was leaving. I'd given my heart and soul to St. Nicholas and now it was time to say goodbye. It was my first job after graduating from the University of Alberta, where I played college football and had centered my academics on sports.

Not surprisingly with my background, I'd spent the last four years coaching almost every school team, from soccer in the fall to track and field in the spring, and teaching the physical education classes as well.

I also taught English, the sex education program (that was interesting), and ran the intramural program. My exceptionally patient and supportive wife, Kathleen, and I lived in a basement suite across from the school. Our place was cramped and dingy but strategically located for a guy who spent his life across the street, blowing his whistle and running around in gym shorts.

There I was sitting on the auditorium stage, the "goodbye" guest of honor in front of the entire school assembly, as the school principal, Henry Czlonka, conducted a number of "end of year" ceremonies. I felt like a lump of sugar slowly dissolving in a glass of Kool-Aid. Doubts about my choice to leave my teaching/coaching position and go on to graduate school at the University of Oregon surfaced more and more as the school year ended. Then Mr. Czlonka said "a few" people wanted to come forward with some "special farewells" and "thanks" to me.

First my team captains came up and gave me "memory gifts," including plaques and trophies with touching messages engraved on them. Other people had a few things to say about my impact and dedication, all very moving on both a personal and professional level.

And then, spontaneously, these crazy, loving kids stood up on their chairs and gave me the ultimate standing ovation. This expression of gratitude was so overwhelming for me that I lost it completely and began to sob like a big, blubbery baby right there in my chair. I did not know what to do, so I just sat with my hands in my face.

Thankfully, the principal quickly adjourned and the students awkwardly shuffled out, a little disquieted by my reaction. I sat there, my face in my hands, until I captured my composure and retreated to my office, which was up the stairs behind the stage. While I huddled in my office, the kids formed what seemed like a never-ending line, each wanting to wish me a personal thanks and goodbye.

I remember one seventh grade boy came up and said, "Mr. Rubis! All I have to give you is my good luck key chain." The boy's key chain turned out to be a little bronze colored medallion; I still have it.

In one moment, these amazing kids gave me a lifetime. I told Kathleen later in the day that it almost didn't matter what happened next in life; whatever comes next would all be a bonus after the outpouring of love and gratitude I experienced that day. In many ways I still feel that way. These incredible kids gave me back way more than they could ever know. If there was a reference for "give and you shall receive," this shining moment was it—and then some—for me.

I share this story because, although it signified the ending of one part of my life, it also meant the beginning of another. Specifically, the experience began to establish for me a belief system for working and contributing. Many of us work without a definitive framework or guide for how we define success. And for many of us, we allow success to be defined exclusively by some combination of position attainment, pay and benefits. While all of these elements are important, many find that these things are insufficient and out of our direct control anyway. We go to work and know something is missing.

Sitting on that stage that day, overcome by emotion, I realized I hadn't just worked with these kids; they had invited me into their domain and allowed me to share what I thought was important. Maybe it was how to hustle on the playing field; maybe it was how to conjugate a verb in English class, or maybe it was simply the idea of doing your best each and every day. Regardless, something magical happened in this relationship between teacher/coach/leader and the "student body." I now thought more purposefully about how I worked and contributed. That was the beginning of framing up and articulating what I now call the **Character Triangle (CT)**.

At the same moment that those kids were thanking me for impacting their lives, I began to establish a playbook for defining personal success at work, and in life. When I first arrived four years earlier at St. Nick's in Edmonton, Alberta, Canada, there was essentially no legacy physical education or sports program. The team uniforms were

3

discolored, mismatched, torn, or missing. We were short of sports equipment in every sense, and our teams were known primarily for losing. By the time I left, we had a school intramural program that fired up every kid from grade four to nine. We were strong competitors and, to the surprise and delight in the community, had even won a few championships in track, basketball, and volleyball. More importantly, the school's academic performance was also improving.

The morale and pride that seemed to be missing in the school four short years earlier, now bounced off the school walls just like the energy of these teenagers. This overall improvement in performance and morale was because of the teamwork of many colleagues and the administration, as well as the willingness of the kids to buy into "the program."

When I look back into the distant mirror, I realize that, as a collective system and culture, the majority of school participants applied the elements of The Character Triangle substantially more than less in our daily "work" at St. Nicholas, and THAT was the fuel that propelled an entire gymnasium of students to stand on their chairs in applause and appreciation. Of course we were not a perfect school and not everyone "liked" everyone else, including me. But collectively, we built something overwhelmingly positive. So I realize *(duh)* some years later, with less of an ego involved in assessing what happened, that the kids were not just cheering me. They were cheering us as an entire system and as collective entities sometimes do; we paused to celebrate and acknowledge each other.

Although there have been no more "chair stands" since leaving St. Nicks, I have experienced a great deal of personal and cultural success in every organization I've worked, and I strongly believe much of this can be directly attributed to a commitment to applying the values resident in The Character Triangle. Of course, I have had my share of personal and cultural failures since then too; and, upon careful reflection, drifting away from these values often contributed to my biggest disappointments.

*So what is the Character Triangle?* I guarantee; it's a personal game changer. *Learning and applying it will help you build more character, have a greater impact, and inspire others.* Change the game by applying the Character Triangle playbook and develop a habit system of using it.

---

***Our character is exclusively ours.***
***We define it by how we think, what we do***
***and the choices we make.***

---

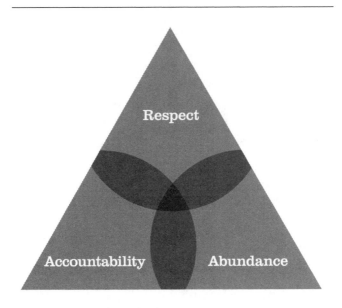

*Figure 1: The Character Triangle © Lorne Rubis*

5

The **Character Triangle** describes and *emphasizes three distinct but interdependent values to apply in our daily thoughts and actions:*

- *Accountability:* Accountability starts with the word "self." When we approach every situation we experience in life by FIRST asking *what* we personally can do about it and *how*[1], we begin to understand the concept of self-accountability. The ideas associated with "blame" and "victim" have little if any place in the self-accountable framework. This is a tricky concept to fully accept and grasp for many of us. We need to ask ourselves daily how often we feel compelled to blame ourselves or others for our condition and circumstances.

- *Respect:* None of us work or, for that matter, live in a vacuum; our successes or failures are all built on the strength of our relationships. And relationships run on respect. To be true to the root of respect, one has to continuously look at one's self with openness and understanding. The point is to examine the way we treat OURSELVES first and then how we treat others. Most of us want to be listened to with understanding, treated with courtesy, and recognized for our contributions. Do we do that with ourselves? Then how much do we do this with others in every interaction? Again, this value can be deceptively oversimplified. I will challenge us on how true we are to this value.

- *Abundance:* Abundant people do not have to take anything away from anyone else to be successful. It is literally fun to work with people who are abundance-focused. They may be competitive but, rather than

---

[1] For more information about the *"What and How"* process, refer to Appendix A.

merely to beat someone, the essence of their drive is to *advance* something. In fact, abundant people relish other's success and achievements. They also focus on the resources available and finding what they need to get results. Generosity of spirit and the belief that giving leads to getting is part of their makeup.

I will elaborate on each of the three inherent elements of the Character Triangle; but for now, the key is attaining a personal understanding and *self-awareness* of each value, and the skill to apply them as a system (which I call a Playbook). Building character, having an impact, and inspiring others means fully embracing these values and applying them relentlessly each day.

Accountability, Respect, and Abundance may sound like straightforward and perhaps even simple concepts; but by the time you finish this book you will think about each value more completely; and, more importantly, you will understand how they connect and reinforce each other to bring you success in all aspects of your life.

Now I have a few questions:

- Do you have a playbook that guides your daily work life and helps you define success at work?

- Are you purposeful and definitive about how you play at work (and at home)?

- Do you have a belief and action roadmap to drive the results you want, or have you been passive and maybe even "sleepwalking" through your work and life routines?

- What is your character?

- How will you make an impact?

- To what extent do you inspire others?

There are some basic facts of life regarding the world of work as many of us have or will experience. Most of us will likely live long enough to work in numerous organizations. Current projections range from ten to fifteen different organizations spanning a thirty-year work life. Most of us will spend approximately 100,000 hours[2] working. Some will be fortunate enough to work in places that are excellent by any number of measures. We are just as likely to be involved with some that we know are just plain lousy.

Many of us will work for and with exceptional as well as crappy managers and leaders. Most workers have little direct control over the company's business model in spite of many leaders' efforts to engage and involve people. The vast numbers will work within predetermined pay and recognition programs with constrained resources to get our jobs done, and little control over whom we work with or where we do our work.

Additionally, in this geo-economic environment of hyper-competition and tornado change, the external buffeting of the organization we reside in can rapidly add to a feeling of little or no personal control over the life cycle of the organization itself, let alone our roles within that organization. The combined effects of these business truisms can leave the best of us dazed, confused, and struggling just to keep our heads above water.

So, the question becomes, how do we go beyond just surviving in this type of undulating work climate? Can we

---

[2] 2080 hours/year (standard number of work hours in a typical business year) for 47 years (starting at age 18 and working to retirement at age 65) equals, 97,760 total hours worked in a typical lifetime.

possibly thrive? Can we be successful? What defines success? Thriving? Can we be successful and have great character too?

Is it possible to complete each day with a personal sense of reward and contribution, regardless of what is happening around us? I believe it is. While we may have less than desirable control of our environment, we do have control of our character—how we choose to think and act, regardless of the situation.

Over the last forty-five years, I have benefited from doing a lot of different things. I've picked up a mop as janitor, slung a sledgehammer as a railway "section man," and packed a lot of bags as a grocery store clerk. I've graded tests as a teacher, created as an entrepreneur, and contributed as a consultant. As a business executive, I have worked directly for the chairman of a public Fortune 50 company, been the COO of a NASDAQ direct marketing firm, and finally took the wheel as CEO of a private company.

I have observed that some individuals manage to achieve personal success and contribute regardless of the situation, the income they are making, or the boss they are working for. These people come in all shapes, sizes, ethnicity, races, education, and at all levels, from front line to corner office.

In some cases, the companies' work environments and business models were successful and perhaps even excellent. In others, the situations were not so great—and some could even be considered pathetic. But in all these scenarios, there were people who lived the elements of the Character Triangle and made a positive difference to their teammates, customers, stakeholders, and others. They weren't always promoted or distinguishable in other ways. Yet they always seemed to work and live with what I describe as character. These people seemed to be the ones who defined their success at work by their personal ethos and approach. Collectively they were impact players, and inspired others by their actions and accomplishments. How did this happen? What were the practices applied? If you're ready, let's answer these questions more completely by taking the Character Triangle from concept to reality.

As you complete *The Character Triangle,* you will be able to determine how valuable and helpful these concepts can be in providing a clear guide and benchmarks. While the values of accountability, respect, and abundance are generic in definition, these values will be exclusively *yours* in application. I make no request that you modify anything about the core of who you are. But I challenge you to observe how well you *really* understand each of these values, whether you consistently apply them, and constructively model and coach others to practice them daily. Like most worthwhile things in life, the rewards and benefits from embracing the Character Triangle will come from regular and incremental practice. Remember—success in any area will most effectively be defined by *you* and your daily interactions with others. If you are lucky, you will experience your own version of a "chair stand" or two.

## Author's Note

As you read this book you will see inserts along the way that relate to the theme of the chapter. These are stories and observations from related work in my blog, www.lornerubis.com. They "ride shotgun" to illustrate and emphasize key learning in the chapter.

At the end of each chapter is a short workbook called the Playbook. I encourage you to journal your observations and actions—to help translate learning into practice and, ultimately, into a habit of how you think and work.

# CHAPTER 2
## BE Accountable

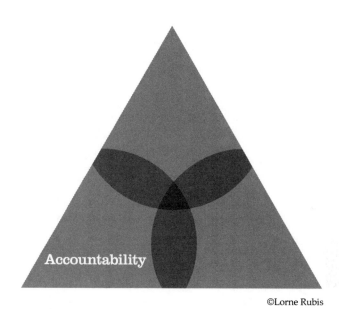

©Lorne Rubis

# Ping the Universe: Will You?

A friend asked to speak to new hires joining a well-regarded company. His task was to give the "newbies" advice regarding making the most of their careers. He asked me what I would tell them, and here is my view:

- Make sure your work is always at the intersection between what you're good at, what you like to do, and what the company needs. Being out of balance in one of those will likely conclude poorly.

- Live the Character Triangle. With all my heart and soul, I believe that connecting and applying the values of accountability, respect, and abundance will allow you to thrive in your career and life. Driving this framework is a lifelong journey for me.

- Define a higher order purpose that arches over whatever you're doing in your life at any time. Your purpose goes well beyond making a living or having a career. It is the "ping" you want to leave in the universe. Defining that is important. Regardless of a change in job or results, and there will likely be many, the higher purpose guides you.

Examine where you are against the three-point checklist above. How are you doing? Which could you work on?

In spite of the economic recession, 2009 managed to serve up one of the biggest sales opportunities in Europe to date. That didn't happen overnight. In fact, I had been close to this opportunity for six months, getting an update from my European managing director almost weekly and, as the decision date zoomed in, daily. Finally, it was coming down to the make-or-break negotiations and I flew to our European offices, along with the chairman of the company, Rud Browne, to make sure we closed a deal that would help us bridge the recession and perhaps redefine our company for the next twenty years.

The flight into Heathrow airport from Seattle ended with its normal shuffle of sleep-deprived passengers descending from every part of the world. While many of my fellow travelers were here on vacation, I was in a hurry to squeeze through passenger control and win this deal.

My company was competing in partnership with a software company and we had never done a deal with them as a consortium before. The win would mean about forty million dollars and, equally important, material sales growth in 2009—quite a feat coming as it was smack dab in the middle of the worst recession since the Great Depression.

In short, we wanted—and needed—this deal. Despite my impatience at the terminal, my confidence level was high. Our team on the ground had done a superb job and positioned us to win. The way I was reading it, I was there mostly to pick up a purchase order. As our team gathered in the offices of the customer on "D day," however, we were a little surprised to hear that the other finalist consortium had made it a price game. At least that's what we were told. We were surprised that there were any further negotiations. Our understanding was that an announcement of the winner was going to be made. *Uh oh*...I detest being surprised.

As the afternoon wore on, it became increasingly clear that the customer was equally happy with the work of the other consortium. Reducing our price was important in order to put our value offering on close-to-equal footing. We still felt as though we were the best match and insiders had hinted (confidentially) that we were indeed the preferred choice.

Negotiations continued through the afternoon under the shared belief that we would eventually prevail. I will never forget the stunned look on the faces of our consortium team when the customer came into our room to tell us that the contract was awarded to our competitors. We were suspended in disbelief, like the audience at the end of a movie that had just delivered a whopper surprise twist ending.

But wait, we hadn't even come close to giving them our best price. How could this have happened? Although I'd certainly lost bids before, this one had gone on so long—with so much riding on it—I literally felt sick to my stomach and thunderstruck by the loss.

As our team stumbled out of that wretched board room into the appropriately gloomy British day, we stood around in a daze, not quite sure what to do next. After a few half-hearted mumbles of "best effort," we drifted to our cars for a long ride back. As I sat in the backseat for that dismal ride, this much was clear: we had lost and, in retrospect, we deserved to lose.

I was on "suicide watch" all weekend. Not really, of course, but I felt terrible and quite a few times imagined this stunning loss as a kind of "business death" from which recovery would be difficult. All that lost effort and investment to win this opportunity sat in the pit of my gut like a giant rock.

*What* I chose to do next and *how* I did it would be critical. The Character Triangle would be tested; that's for sure.

## "Why is this happening to ME?"

What is your understanding of the concept of accountability? My experience is that people often think of accountability as a concept best applied to others. "Holding other people accountable" is a common phrase. In business, I guess you could say it even qualifies as a buzz term, something we often see in mission and vision statements. How often have you heard or considered that someone needs to "hold others accountable"? This approach to accountability may be limiting and, perhaps, even counterproductive.

While it is vital that we all be held accountable, continually putting the emphasis on others merely takes the spotlight off ourselves and *our* responsibilities. From my perspective, being ***self-accountable*** is a much more constructive way to live and work.

I appreciate and, in fact, welcome the idea of someone assigning me responsibilities and having high expectations that I take care of those responsibilities well; but I am most attracted to the idea of holding ***myself*** **accountable**. This self-accountability applies not just to some areas of work and home life (for instance, those I'm best at or most comfortable with), but in *all* areas of work and home life. The very foundation of self-accountability revolves around the notion of taking personal responsibility for whatever situation you are in: good, bad, or ugly.

## Kick 'Em You Know Where

Thomas L. Friedman, *NYT* columnist and author of *The World is Flat*, wrote an interesting piece in his June 11, 2010, Sunday "Week in Review" op-ed. He refers to a personal letter by a friend of Tom's, sent to the editor of *The Beaufort Gazette* in South Carolina, which states essentially that the Gulf Spill ultimately comes from choices you and I make. Blaming BP, the government or any other group for the macro issue distracts us from determining the root cause and moving forward. That may sound ridiculous when we think about how far removed the vast majority of us are from drilling a well thousands of feet deep.

However, we the people established the conditions where we frankly have been and continue to be committed to living off the cheapest oil we can get as our primary source of energy. Of course we expect people to execute the energy supply chain responsibly, but our unwillingness to really change the oil paradigm is a bilateral fact. Friedman makes the self-accountability argument. We need to take control over what and how we personally take action. Some of it is smaller and in our immediate sphere (e.g. getting rid of our gas guzzlers, planting a garden, supporting the buy local/ slow money initiatives). Other action is less direct but equally important, demanding that we pass an energy reform bill that dramatically reduces dependence on Mideast oil. This is not a political argument for one thing or another but a plea for self-accountability and forward action. Blame by itself changes nothing and we end up getting kicked where it hurts.

---

*"Turning our thinking around and asking more personally accountable questions is one of the most powerful and effective things we can do to improve our organizations and our lives."*
— John Miller, QBQ

---

I think this is a powerful way to act and approach every situation. Think for a moment and sincerely ask yourself, rather than immediately pointing the finger at someone else, wouldn't it be more effective and productive if you approached your challenges at work (and life) *first* by asking and answering the questions: *what way* and *how **you*** personally might make a difference?

So, be first. Ask what you can do about a situation and answer how you might do something about it.

Consider:

- How do you think your boss or teammate would respond if you seriously and sincerely addressed a problem from this perspective?

- Would it make a difference how you might work together?

- Would it pave the road to exploring better ways of mutually winning versus the corporate duel of thrust and defend?

- Would it make you a better team player?

- Possibly a better team leader?

## Why the Blame Game Never Works

If our company has disappointing quarterly sales results, I have a responsibility to address the situation **with a sense of urgency** to help drive better results ASAP. I recognize this isn't SOP (standard operating procedure) at every company. In fact, a relatively simplistic and straightforward approach is to "hold the VP of sales accountable." After all, I am the CEO; managing quarterly sales isn't directly in my job description—but it *IS* in hers.

I could simply call her into my office and find out what she plans to do about this. Perhaps a sterner and more "CEO-like" approach to the situation might get the better response. I could even subtly—or not-so-subtly—threaten her just a little by "putting a little fire under her feet." A little fear and intimidation is a tried-and-true form of executive motivation. Anyone with a title, and authority over pay and position, can get real good at this technique real fast.

Of course, it would be expected under these circumstances for the VP of sales to attend my meeting with a kneejerk, finger-pointing, blame-game explanation of (amongst many things) "how bad the market is," "how we are actually out-performing some competitors," "how production was late with product releases," the "underperformance of a few top sales people," etc., etc. The blame first—assume responsibility last, duel can become interesting. Although, as the boss, I do have the "bigger weapon."

Obviously, I am over-simplifying the interaction to make a point. That point being that neither of us in the above scenario—not me, the CEO, or her (the VP of sales) is innocent in playing the blame game; I immediately blamed her and she, in turn, quickly and efficiently blamed a host of others. Hey, everybody's doing it! Why not us, right?

However, what if the VP of sales AND I both approached the situation with a serious self-examination around *what* and *how* we might personally do things better to improve results? As an example, I could be a better leader and coach, both to the VP of sales and her staff.

I could, for instance, personally help close deals with top prospects, provide resources for a new marketing campaign, amend the value proposition, etc. In turn, the VP of sales might suggest ways she could improve the sales management system, better mine our customer database, get out with our top customers more, examine win/loss changes, or drive more sales activity with the most profitable segments, etc.

If we both have the self-accountability approach and skill to aim and fire at data, issues, problems, and behaviors, rather than a personal test to see "who can out-blame the other," the "duel" in this case becomes instead a "joint assault" on changing process and results. This is fundamentally different, for both sides, than feeling victimized and blaming. Of course, this approach is not necessarily easier.

Blaming? Now that's easier. With a simple finger point in somebody else's direction, it's no longer my fault, nor my responsibility. Instead, when we first take personal accountability seriously, we each have to skillfully analyze and execute on appropriate actions. As we all know, this takes additional time, thought, and energy. However, despite its greater degree of difficulty, the tone of the interaction between us changes substantially.

Typically, this focus is much more positive, with interpersonal energy better applied to each of us contributing personal and forward-moving action. The opposite results in less productive, defensive behavior, which is energy draining, often leading to interpersonal friction. If results

## Crises and Blame

The 2010 Louisiana Gulf oil crisis is a classic example of blame becoming a barrier and detriment to the solution. Blame cannot cap the well. All groups working together eventually did: BP, Coast Guard, EPA, and local groups. All ideally wanted the same thing—cap the damn well and stop the environmental damage. Worry about all the litigious action likely to follow later. Lawsuits won't kill the environment; weeks of spewing oil will.

Often under times of crisis, *blame* seems to become the driving agenda between interdependent parties. Yet the immediate mandate must be to find the solution not the hollow *victory* of proving somebody *wrong*. There is a time for reviewing what happened after the problem is solved. Leadership is bringing all parties who can add value to the table, listening with an open mind, and having the courage to make choices and act. The same principles apply to the small crises many of us are involved with regularly. See what you can do to focus on the problem and suppress the seduction to blame. You will find yourself working on the right things in the right way. Hopefully learning this principle by all parties involved in the Gulf fiasco will improve problem solving for the next time because there will be a "next time."

do not change, I still might have to replace my sales leader one day (that is the great unspoken, regardless of how much personal accountability she and I take). But I guarantee you that the chances of succeeding improve greatly if the VP of sales and I take a self-accountable approach versus playing the blame game.

Acting with character has a lot to do with our approach to an issue. We may not always succeed, but there is a certain level of winning from doing things the Character Triangle way. If things don't work out, and each of us has done our personal best, then we can each hold our heads up high. If I put the burden exclusively on the VP of sales without asking *what, how,* and *when* I could have helped to change results, I will have underserved her as a leader—and myself as a CEO. If she does the same, she has allowed herself to be victimized—or become a martyr.

---

### Dig a Little Deeper and Find a Well!

Do you sometimes want to change things? Wish *They* would do something to make things different? What if the *They* were you?

Ryan Hreljac was nineteen years old in 2010 when I discovered his story, but this Canadian teenager was inspired at age seven to raise seventy dollars through doing extra chores to help build wells in Africa. In the twelve years since, his own charity, Ryan's Wells Foundation, has helped fund more than 550 wells in sixteen countries. He has helped supply clean water to 700,000 people.

Sometimes it is a matter of asking what and how you can take action to change things. Self-accountability is the courage and confidence to believe you can do something to develop a more desired state of being. This applies at work and outside of work. Each of us has way more power and influence than we often believe. Start now...before you know it, 700,000 people have clean drinking water. Start now... your place of work will see the benefit of changes you have initiated.

---

## Key Steps to Becoming More Accountable

Being Accountable does not mean blaming oneself, either. This exercise is not designed to take the blame off of everyone else and put it squarely on our own shoulders. The entire concept of blame is not very helpful, whether pointing at others or ourselves. When the concept of self-accountability is first introduced or revisited, some people rush to "fall on their swords" to demonstrate self-accountability. This is not helpful and, frankly, can come across as disingenuous. Regardless of how it appears, the effect is the same: blame decreases effectiveness, not increases it.

When we're busy blaming, be it others or ourselves, that means we aren't busy finding solutions. We are only identifying those who may have gotten us into trouble. If sales are down it is absolutely critical to find out why, but only in the sense that we can correct it via practical and effective solutions. Self-responsibility is forward motion; blame takes us backward.

How to avoid the blame game in your own life? It can be a hard habit to break, but with the following four steps you, too, can leave the blame game in the past and look forward to a life full of personal accountability:

1.  **Be honest and do it now! Get the data and recognize and accept that a situation is not acceptable.** Avoidance is often a signal that something is wrong. Be aware of that, and insist on an honest evaluation. Get the facts and data you need to define the problem. If sales are down, developing and executing on a plan for getting sales back up is a forward-motion step we can take immediately. It includes discovering why sales were down; indeed, knowing "why" sales were down is necessary to help in determining "how" to get them back up. But making

plans for a more desirable outcome immediately takes precedence over the blame game.

2. **Be first. Ask yourself in advance of expecting anything from others, *what* and *how*[3] you personally might do to change things.** The emphasis here is on what YOU can do, FIRST and foremost, even before you consider what someone else might do to help. Again, these are habitual behaviors that need to be retrained; and when you learn to start every solution with yourself, this habit becomes more and more natural over time.

3. **Do what you can do. Take personal action to improve process and results. Be careful not to underestimate the plan.** The solution starts with you. You will often need others to accomplish the mission, but whether you're the CEO, VP of sales, leader, manager, or team member, you can still have a direct impact on the larger organization's results when you take personal action to improve both the process and the results. Don't wait for others to make the first move. Move forward. However be careful of underestimating what is going to be required to make things better. The execution is in the details of the plan.

4. **Do not "beat yourself up."** Being self-accountable does not involve blame, including self-blame. Acting with character is a lifelong process, not an overnight achievement and the only way to learn is to grow.

When starting to approach accountability as a personal matter, it can also be disappointing—and even frustrating—when others do not reciprocate. In fact, it is often downright exasperating when others listen to your self-accountable

---

[3] Refer to Appendix A for more information about "What and How."

approach and choose not to act in kind. In fact, in many cases being responsible for your own actions could unwittingly result in others taking less responsibility for their actions! However, it is important to apply **self-accountability as a personal value in your character**, regardless of the behavior of others. This may feel somewhat counter-intuitive, but remember: this is about defining your own success by living with character. It is often a slow burn but eventually people get it and will start modeling your behavior.

It is more efficient and effective when others share this value and approach to working together, but the more important consideration is, first and foremost, **how *you* behave.** Often asking what others might do about a situation or behavior can facilitate their self-reflection. Yet applying self-accountability is not a matter of whether others do it or not. It is about **who *you* are** and **what *you* stand for** as a leader in work and life, regardless of job title or position.

Just as importantly, remember too that others often learn when you lead by example. Not everyone, though. Some will simply never take personal accountability for their actions, on the job site or at home. But in most organizations your team takes its cues from you, and as you begin to evidence more self-responsibility they will, too.

## Do You Know Someone Like Sam?

Sam is a very effective salesperson. He is faced with challenging markets, tough competitors, variable quality and service from operations, some great and not so great marketing, pricing, etc. He believes in the offering he sells and knows the company he works for, like all companies, has strengths and shortcomings.

When Sam meets with his boss, he comes prepared by

outlining all the things he can do within his control to achieve better results. He does have requests and suggestions from his boss and other departments, but he always starts with what he can contribute first.

Sam has come to the conclusion that when he has perfected his personal sales process, he will then be able to devote time to running other people and departments as well. Though he doesn't hold that title just yet, like many good leaders Sam is tough-minded and respectfully committed to constructively improving processes and behaviors of others who may be unproductive. **But he always starts with improving himself first.**

Self-accountability isn't just a job requirement for Sam; it's a matter of character. He is self-demanding, has high performance expectations, and is a great guy to have on the team. Of course, Sam is also very *respectful* in his approach and has an *abundance* perspective (more to come on these values in the next chapters).

## Do You Know Someone Like Jim?

Jim is frustrated. He believes that he is a successful salesperson **in spite of the company he works for.** Jim often thinks to himself, *It is unbelievable how screwed up things are around here!* The sales management is somewhat of a joke, according to Jim. They don't know where they are going at the top of the organization. If production had better delivery, Jim feels, he could meet customer expectations more often.

The sales commission program is broken. When are they going to fix the darn thing? The head of marketing is a "slob" and, to Jim's way of thinking, should have been fired "years ago." The only way the marketing head still has his job, Jim figures, is because he obviously has "pictures of somebody at the top."

Jim starts meetings with his sales leader by giving her an earful of, "What's screwed up?" In fact, lately Jim has come to the conclusion that complaining about things is not really worth it. No one bothers to listen anyway. They just care about lining their pockets.

Jim is tough-minded and at a point in his life where he is not putting up with incompetence. Regardless of who they are, what division, or how high up, Jim is not afraid to tell *them* that *they* suck when the opportunity presents itself. Jim has come to the conclusion that if everyone worked as hard as he did, and cared a lot more about customers, things would be a lot better. He enjoys getting together with a couple of other straight-talking people in the company who know "what's up." It is reassuring for Jim to have others recognize that people at the top and other departments don't know up from down. When other people "get it right," Jim will finally hit the sales numbers his personal hard work deserves. Pointing out how other people should be accountable is a matter of Jim's character.

## So Much of How We Choose to Act
## is Under Our Personal Control

Sam and Jim are very real, summary composites of people I've worked with over the years. You may recognize one or both in your company as well. They both can "sell," but there is a fundamental difference in their contribution to the organization. Sam is very self-accountable. When you work with Sam, you know that the approach is going to be constructive. Most of all, Sam recognizes that *he is the person most responsible for the results he achieves.*

Sure, the contributions from others can and always

could get better. But Sam goes home most days self-defining success and contribution according to his own definition of (self) success and failure. Meanwhile, Jim really does feel that "others are to blame" when things go wrong. He is constantly demanding that others do things to change, to grow, to learn, to adapt, but is so frustrated and even angry from to time to time with their lack of performance that he fails even to consider his own. Regardless of evidence to the contrary, Jim genuinely believes that improvements are most needed elsewhere.

Would you believe that Sam and Jim both work in the same company? Not only that, both have the capability to approach their work life with a perspective that is directionally toward or away from self-accountability. My experience is that people who approach their work life by asking and answering the *what* and *how* self-accountability questions—i.e. **"What can I do to change/improve?"** and **"How can I change/improve my own performance?"**—will be more successful and, what's more, find their work life more rewarding.

Imagine an organization populated by one group more than the other. The effects would either be revitalizing or demoralizing. What if you were in an organization where literally everyone interacted in a self-accountable way, like Sam? Could you see how potentially positive a sales force this could be, when from the top down every leader, manager, and employee started with the "what" and "how" self-accountability questions first? Self-accountability alone does not drive sales, but if every salesperson had the same attitude as Sam's, the likelihood of increased sales goes up dramatically.

Now imagine the opposite scenario, where a workplace

full of Jims went around starting every sales meeting with a complaint and approached every job as if everyone else were incompetent. Jim may be a hard-charging, self-starting salesperson, but if he can't be a positive team player who at least considers the fact that he's not perfect, he will never contribute significantly to the organization—in sales or elsewhere. Neither will anyone else if they, too, share Jim's "blame game" attitude.

None of us are perfect and, from time to time, it is hard not to feel a little victimized by fellow employees, by competitors, by clients, by customers, even by our own management and leadership. **But so much of how we choose to act is under our personal control.** Regardless of what role or position you have in the organization, people will come to know you as a person who approaches challenges from a position of personal strength and contribution if you **consistently and genuinely take a self-accountable stance.**

---

### The Foolish Seduction of "Free Fall" Complaining

This is a perspective from a CEO who has spent a career thinking about leadership, accountability, and problem solving. Some people in organizations think about problem solving as a pitch and catch process. It is similar to jumping off a fifty-story building and feeling like we're flying for the first forty-nine floors. Of course the landing changes that perspective. When we participate in an exercise aimed at developing a list of complaints and concerns, it might feel really good while we're doing it...almost like we're flying. I have been part of these kinds of meetings where making lists of problems and concerns has an incredible momentary high.

---

But like the jumping metaphor, the landing is the same. Why?

Complaining and developing lists of concerns, as a unilateral exercise, usually just results in problems being shifted around. Well-intended managers often think this is great leadership but unwittingly end up shouldering the list of problems on their own. Of course most often they cannot solve the problems unilaterally. In the same way, well-intended employees do a *"problem dump"* (a.k.a. a bitch session) and feel good until the bloom falls off the cathartic rose. We can become bitterly disappointed when the problem list remains mostly unchanged over a period of time. We hear phrases like, "Why didn't they...?"

Self-accountability always involves bringing a personal contribution to solving problems. Hit and run, or pitch and catch, problem dumping is usually counterproductive. Resist problem identification as a singular activity. It usually promotes organizations to become better at making lists than taking action. If we want to drive a meaningful problem-solving process, each of us has to come to a problem or issue with a contribution in hand. The fix is almost always a collective connection of those impacted and involved.

I look for people who are self-accountable problem solvers, not problem dumpers or collectors. How would you identify yourself?

Remember the story I used to open this chapter, about my ill-fated trip to Europe after six long months of behind-the-scenes work? So, what happened on the European deal? Well, once we'd all recovered from the initial shock of losing the account, the very first thing we did was to immediately try to win it back. Our chairman was particularly heroic all weekend; but regardless of how hard we tried, or for how long, it was all too little, too late. When we finally realized (you might say *admitted*) we could not win, we just as quickly went into self-accountability learning mode. We followed the key steps outlined above.

I personally led learning sessions with our customer, our software partner, and internally. I started by asking "what" and "how" I could have been more effective as a CEO in leading this to a winning outcome. Each person subsequently did the same in what turned out to be an extremely challenging, yet ultimately rewarding, exercise.

As seductive as it was, we genuinely tried as hard as we could not to blame and there was a lot of "gun powder" around to do so; that is, if we had allowed ourselves to deteriorate to that level. It was my—and our—responsibility to get the most out of this situation, not the least. Being self-accountable is definitely being tough in assessing what happened. Getting the data on the table involves confidence and honesty. We were relentless in attacking the processes that didn't work. And I am proud to say that we are a better company for it in many ways. We hate losing, but we did and there was no way around that, no matter how hard we tried to salvage the situation. Instead we worked our tails off in learning and applying every possible lesson that we could to turn that loss into a win.

I believe that, if I would have been in the "I am going

to hold others accountable" mode and started reprimanding people at that point (which was certainly an understandable way to feel), I would have done more harm to the organization than the lost account in the first place. More importantly, I had to set the example of self-accountability. And I benefited from colleagues who took the same approach.

To that end, I used the Accountability Playbook.

In the latter part of 2010, we won a breakthrough contract in the United Kingdom, using the learning from the painful loss described above. It is now the template we are using to drive over thirty percent of our business. Applying learning from mistakes is a glorious thing!

 **The Be Accountable Playbook**

Here is the first page of your CT Playbook for being Accountable. Use it wisely and don't delay; start with one "play" and add the others as they come naturally to you. Remember, these are habitual behaviors so they will take some time to adopt, but don't stop until you've mastered the entire list.

**1.0 Establish the mindset to improve yourself first.** Approach issues with self-examination of in *what* way and *how* you might contribute before asking or expecting from others.

**2.0 Always ask in *what* way and *how* you might do something.** Begin each interaction with yourself in control by taking responsibility for your action.

**3.0 Act self-accountable without expecting reciprocity.** Being accountable is more about your character than others. You can be self-accountable regardless of what others do.

**4.0 Avoid blaming, especially self-blaming.** There is very little value, if any, in finding someone to blame. Remember that blame moves you backward while holding yourself accountable moves your forward.

**5.0 Watch out for the "victim thinking" often related to the word "they."** Waiting or wanting the often undefined or mysterious "they" to make things better is often frustrating for all, to say nothing of "wishful thinking."

**6.0 Be on the lookout for the "procrastination" signal and under-planning.** Avoidance often is a signal that you're waiting for someone to do something. At the same time taking action does not imply capricious activity. It takes a plan and be cautious not to underestimate what is needed to make a sustainable difference.

---

**Feedback in Today's Workplace**

I have always found annual performance reviews almost useless. If we wait to get and give performance feedback 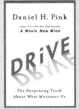 on an annual basis, it must not matter much. I want to give and get feedback in a much more timely way. Dan Pink, author of *Drive: The Surprising Truth about What Motivates Us,* publishes a weekly article in the Telegraph UK and his November 6, 2010, article[4] was right on. He suggests three things we can do to make a workplace a little more feedback rich:

1. Do it ourselves. Why not establish our own feedback system? Get feedback on a regular basis (once per month?) from colleagues on how we're doing. If we have a boss who's really thinking clearly, that person will honor and support this activity.

2. Peer Recognition. I'm a big fan of people giving each other recognition. In the company I run, people are encouraged to send each other written acknowledgments on a card we call an "ACE" card. In Pink's article he references a large American engineering firm where employees also have the green light to award team members fifty-dollar gift certificates.

3. Do it with software. There are some great software packages that drive extensive 360-degree feedback—the more timely, specific, and constructive, the more effective results.

Great leading companies have feedback systems driving behavior. Self-accountable people find a way to get timely feedback on our performance.

---

[4] http://www.telegraph.co.uk/finance/jobs/8113600/Think-Tank-Fix-the-workplace-not-the-workers.html (Accessed March 10, 2011)

## Practice the Plays

Now that you've studied the Playbook, here is an opportunity to practice the plays themselves. Take the following actions and journal them below:

✔ Observe situations where you or others default to using the "they" word regarding work (or life) activities you are involved with.

_____

_____

_____

_____

_____

✔ Observe situations where time is spent on blaming or defending versus constructive problem solving.

_____

_____

_____

_____

_____

✔ Observe self-accountable people who already approach issues by offering actions they personally might take to make it better. How effective are they?

_____

_____

_____

_____

_____

✔ Look for work situations where you identify an issue and propose to people impacted how and what you might do to make it better, without asking for anything from anyone else. Observe the reaction and dialogue that follows.

_____

_____

_____

_____

✔ Identify and plan for one or two situations where you will apply the principles in this chapter.

_____

_____

_____

_____

_____

↗ Journal how effective the outcome was? What worked well? What didn't? What did you learn?

_____

_____

_____

_____

_____

↗ Make this approach a way of life and personal character to you regardless of how others embrace the concept. Do not expect anything other than a greater feeling of contribution and control in return. The return on investment to your character is immediate.

_____

_____

_____

_____

_____

# Personal Learning on Being Accountable

## You're the Boss with Your Boss

*Remember: you are as responsible for the relationship with your boss as your boss is with you.*

*Being the Boss: The Three Imperitives for Becoming a Great Leader*, co-authored by Harvard professor Linda A. Hill and executive Kent Lineback, was picked by a number of critics as a 2010 superb book to read if one wants to advance their career. The book covers three core areas: manage yourself, manage your network, and manage your team. There are many outstanding insights in the book, and I want to highlight one of the perspectives. Many people I have worked with complain about the shortcomings of their bosses, and put most of the burden for the status of relationship on them. Professor Hill brings a view that is valuable to reflect on:

"It's common to let the person up the chain be most responsible for whether you have a healthy relationship, but you're equally responsible. If you don't manage that relationship right, your team is not going to be able to do what it needs to do.

Powerlessness corrupts as much as power. You shouldn't feel powerless with your boss. That's not the deal. You have to figure out the sources of power you have to influence the boss. You also have to see the boss as human and fallible in all the ways that you're human and fallible, and figure out how to deal with the reality of who that person is—rather than the ideal of what you'd like that person to be like. There are really bad bosses, and you can't be naive or cynical about this. It's hard to be successful with a bad boss, and sometimes success means figuring out how to get out of that situation. But before you decide that's the deal, you need to take responsibility for the relationship, because it's definitely two-way.

Many people have multiple bosses, and we also discuss the challenges there. One of the most common missteps is to deal with the boss who's closest to you physically and treat your relationship with your other boss as out of sight, out of mind. So we talk about how you have to manage the priorities between those two bosses and how to negotiate what will be your priorities, given their priorities."

Take honest stock of what we're doing to improve the relationship with our boss, or bosses.

I became the VP of Operations of the Los Angeles Kings Hockey Club at a time when Phil Anschutz, the brilliant billionaire, took over the club as the "anchor tenant" of what has now become the very successful Anschutz Entertainment Company. I loved the job and was excited about the prospects from a career perspective. It was a combination of two things I had a great deal of passion for: leadership and sports/entertainment.

I was one of a handful of people in a private room at the Peninsula Hotel in Los Angeles, with the Anschutz and Roski families (Ed Roski was Phil's partner in this venture) when a model of what was to become Staples Center was first unveiled. It was a privilege to see the excitement of those involved. Entertainment in Los Angeles was about to get a great new venue.

The president of the company, Tim Lieweke (who I believe is one of the most effective and capable sports entertainment executives anywhere), and I got off to a great start. However, for a number of reasons at the end of our first year of working together, we seemed to end up competing against rather that helping each other. I felt that he was being unreasonable, unfair, and even disrespectful to me and most of the other people who worked in the organization. I can say that for the first time in my career, I was in a situation where I felt that I was in conflict with my boss. Moreover, I was feeling victimized.

Here I was working my tail off, believing that I was making a positive contribution to the success of the organization, and all I seemed to get for my considerable effort and great results was grief from "my boss." I started to feel sorry for myself and spent more time confirming with others that I was "right" and he was "wrong." I was living the blame game big-time.

In retrospect, this might sound hopelessly naïve and foolish. However, when one is in the middle of these circumstances, it is less obvious than when one examines pulling away and seeing the experience "in the rearview mirror." If I would have better applied the Character Triangle at the time, I think I would have managed the situation differently. Rather than spending my time feeling and acting like a victim, confirming with others that I was "right" and he was "wrong," I would have spent more time thinking about in *what* way and *how* I might do things differently.

Furthermore, I would have been better skilled at constructively confronting and discussing this situation with Tim. In retrospect, perhaps, things wouldn't have improved, and Tim and I might have never really fired on all cylinders. But I chose to leave without fully applying the Character Triangle and working fully with Character.

Tim and I have met a few times since. He has always been gracious and our meetings have been very cordial. He has gone on to build a powerful and hugely successful sports entertainment empire under the AEG brand. I learned a lot from him.

By applying more self-accountability, I might have used a different thought process and taken different courses of action. One way or another I would have looked in the mirror, knowing that I gave it my best shot by doing everything. I thought I did at the time.

Back then I didn't have the skill and insight to manage the situation as effectively as I would have today with the Character Triangle taking up more residence in my soul. As it was, I ended up leaving the sports organization to take a VP of sales job with a public company. This would become a great experience in its own right.

---

### Do You Know How to Apologize?

Dr. Aaron Lazare, author of the book *On Apology,* underscores the importance of genuinely apologizing as an important human act, allowing for those that are wrong to repent and for those that have been wronged to forgive. Management and leadership guru, Tom Peters, talks about sincerely saying "sorry" as one of top leaders' most important attributes. But do we really know and understand this act of contrition or are some of us inclined to throw out the "S" word with a hope that we can make the issue go away.

The data says that platitudes and "non–apology apologies" are worse than no apology at all. For example, one poll shows that only fifty-four percent of respondents felt that Tiger Woods apology (for his marital indiscretions) was sincere. Lisa Belkin wrote a great *NYT Magazine* article[5] entitled "Why Is It So Hard to Apologize Well." She refers to research by Jennifer Robbennolt, a professor of law and psychology at the University of Illinois.

"Dr. Robbennolt presented test subjects with a hypothetical situation—one in which a cyclist injures a pedestrian. She then attributed one of three statements to the cyclist and asked the subjects whether the injured party should accept a proffered settlement. When a full apology was offered ("I am so sorry that you were hurt. The accident was all my fault, I was going too fast and not watching where I was going"), seventy-three percent of the respondents said the pedestrian should be willing to accept the settlement. When no apology was offered, fifty-two percent said the pedestrian should settle. And when only a partial apology was offered ("I am so sorry that you were hurt, and I really hope that you feel better soon"), thirty-five percent opted for a settlement."

Do you think Tony Hayward, then-CEO of BP, was sincere in his apology (regarding the enormous oil spill in the Gulf)?

So here are the essential self-accountable guidelines for apologizing at work (or anywhere):

1. Be honest enough to recognize when we have screwed up, and admit it.

2. Sincerely express regret regarding our behavior and consequences.

3. Take full responsibility for our behavior/actions (even when we think there are extenuating circumstances).

4. State the learning and plan to act differently; outline how to prevent it from occurring again.

5. Ask for forgiveness.

---

[5] http://www.nytimes.com/2010/07/04/magazine/04fob-wwln-t.html?_r=1 (Accessed March 7, 2011)

I like the way Belkin concludes her article: when an apology fails, two things are lost—the victims are not asked for forgiveness, nor are they given a chance to grant it. Being asked to forgive restores dignity to the injured. Granting forgiveness is a step toward moving on. A botched apology not only taints the act of apology but the ability to accept an apology as well. And that is unforgivable.

Let's be self-accountable...apologize when we screw up...do it the right way and go forward.

At Zones, Inc., where I became the VP of sales and then COO, the market began to dramatically change and we had to evolve from a consumer-based catalogue company to a "business to business" direct marketing company. The transition was difficult because the entire business model required changing. In this case, we found ourselves under enormous financial pressure. By taking an aggressive "what and how" approach, I knew that we needed to achieve some major win to positively impact our long-term viability.

This thinking was the basis for personally leading a team to successfully win an IT fulfillment contract with Microsoft worth over one hundred million dollars in annual revenue. I remember bringing a group of "Zoners" together, a number who doubted we could pull off a project of this scale, and asking people to focus on in *what* way and *how* each of us could win this versus "why" we couldn't. By getting everyone to focus on their personal *what* and *how*, **we did it**. Many people familiar with the situation believe that Microsoft deal provided Zones with much-needed revenue and the creatibility bridge to successfully complete the transition to a business to business (B to B) direct marketer.

## Forgiveness: The Ed Thomas Story

Ed Thomas was the high school football coach of the Aplington-Parkersburg (Iowa) Falcons. In 2008, Coach Thomas rallied the town of 1,800 to overcome a devastating tornado that ripped through the community that June. They played football in the fall of 2008, against all odds, and went 11 and 1. The Falcons were a conduit for the Aplington-Parkersburg area moving forward to rebuild. Coach Thomas was a key leader in making it happen.

On June 14, 2010, at the ESPY awards, the Thomas family received the Arthur Ashe award for courage. Why? On June 24, 2009, a psychologically disturbed ex-player shot and killed Coach Ed Thomas. This tragedy tore at the fabric of the community. Yet due to the lifetime belief and example of forgiveness set by Ed, the Thomas family led by wife Jan forgave the killer and his family first. They then used the power of forgiveness to move forward.

In this case ordinary people were dragged into an extraordinary situation. But when you learn about Ed Thomas and family, you realize their faith and belief in forgiveness is extraordinary.

If the Thomas family can forgive a man and his family for the killing of their patriarch, can we forgive under less daunting and extreme cases? I think we can. Forgiving is an act of abundance. It is the total opposite of scarcity.

Now to bring it to the workplace: do we have the ability to forgive transgressions that are not about life or death at work? The obvious answer must be yes. So, let's all work to forgive that one person we've been mad at. It is normally an uplifting experience for the forgiver and forgiven. Be accountable. Start now.

Both situations above are different in scale and scope. However, what is also different is the **approach in thinking.** I have discovered through much trial and error that, whenever I have applied the self-accountability value, the outcome has been more fruitful. More importantly, I am in **more in control of the result when I apply the self-accountability playbook.** Life does not always roll out the way we want it to, but my deep belief is that if we take the "what and how I can" approach, we live our lives with more character. As a result, we have more power over the outcome. Of course, the outcome may vary, but we can genuinely move forward more constructively, knowing we have been in the game acting with Character.

When I find myself blaming someone else or pointing the finger, my self-accountability alarm rings with a big "bong." It still goes off, but a lot less than in the past. I'm getting better at establishing the mindset to look at myself first and asking the right questions that stem from that view.

---

*"Things I read on employee surveys: 'It's not my job… No one told me… It couldn't be helped… It's not my fault… When are they going to do something about it…?'"*
— Lorne Rubis

---

# CHAPTER 3
# BE Respectful

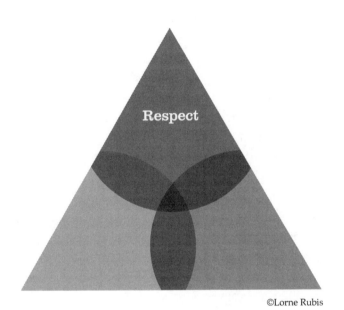

©Lorne Rubis

## It's About Who You KNOW, not WHO You Know

Mother Theresa said that the most terrible poverty was loneliness and feeling unloved. I wonder how lonely and isolated people feel in Western culture.

One day last fall my wife and I dropped in on a hip coffee house in the Eastlake area of Seattle. Eighteen people, most in their twenties and thirties, sat by themselves plugged into laptops (16 Apple, 1 iPad, 1 PC...hmm). There was another couple our age; he was on his Blackberry and she was on her cell phone. Okay, it's just an observation, but I wonder if our work environment is taking on added importance as a place for face-to-face personal interaction. My message is around the importance of getting to really know the people we work with. It is so important to care about each other. Yes, it's work, but work is a huge part of our life.

I took time to learn about the life of one of our tech supervisors. Holy cow—what a story...escaping the Cambodian Killing Fields, three days and nights at sea, crossing as one of the Vietnamese boat people, and more. There is no way I could fully appreciate this man without learning about his life.

Please take the time to unplug once in a while. Learn about the people who work around you, and be thankful for those that care and get to know you.

Sometimes it takes an objective, outside pair of eyes to determine whether or not the organizations we belong to have more or less of a respectful—or disrespectful—atmosphere. When I first became president of Ryzex, I noticed personal attacks creeping into some meetings and other daily interactions.

Every company experiences tension from time to time. I was concerned about the mean-spirited behavior I observed. If an organization is to be successful, it must have an atmosphere of respectful listening and open dialogue. Conflict and disagreement are necessary, but it must be constructive and respectful.

A winning business culture needs to be tough-minded, competitive and, as discussed in Chapter 1, very accountable. However, fear of personal attack must be expunged or the organization becomes riddled with fear and devolves into a poisoned culture of bullying and other destructive behavior.

In my first month on the job a number of sales people expressed concern to me about the abusive behavior of a certain sales engineer. The engineer in question would literally berate these team members on the phone, telling them how "stupid" and "incompetent" they were, etc. I collected facts and data on this situation and brought in the engineer and his boss to express my concerns. It was also important to address the engineer with respect. I focused on his behavior and did my best to engage him in understanding why it was abusive and unconstructive. (I also listened to his concerns about the repetitive annoying calls.) I asked the sales engineer and his boss to outline the consequences of continuing this unacceptable behavior, to themselves, to others, to the sales process, and to the company as a whole. We agreed on what specific things each of us could do to stop this abusive interaction. This included my commitment to work with the sales department and taking action to minimize contacting engineering with trivial, annoying questions (He had a good point on this). The answers to many of the questions aimed at engineering were easily accessible by other means. So we agreed, and everyone in the room had an improvement action plan, but I also explained that while it would take time to change Sales' behavior, the one thing that was unacceptable, over and above any technical problems we'd just discussed, were the twin issues of personal attack and abuse.

In no uncertain terms I explained that there was "no second chance" for this type of disrespectful behavior and that the next step was dismissal "if it happened again." So I was understandably disappointed and frustrated when, only a day later, I walked into the engineering office and heard this same guy telling the person on the other end of the phone what an idiot he was.

Clearly, this was what best-selling leadership author, Tom Peters, and others call "a moment of truth" for me, for this employee, and for the company. After all, we had just spent considerable time working on an agreed to action plan, with a clear and written understanding that on matters of personal abuse, there would be no second chances. Now, not only had I heard of this type of behavior again, but I had heard it—firsthand.

After a short investigation, we fired the guy that very day. I explained to the entire company that one sure way to be invited to leave the company was to abuse someone else. In fact, I wanted us to get much better at dialogue and listening, as a rule, and not just when I was walking around. It's important to remember that respect does not mean never voicing an opinion, only doing so respectfully. Disagreement and heated debates were okay, even welcome; but from now on we were going to manage ourselves in a respectful manner as a way of conducting daily business.

It may be ironic and somewhat unfortunate to choose a story about firing someone to introduce the topic of respect. But taking this action cleared the way for a whole lot of gain when it came to becoming a more respectful organization. I'm not sure folks would have been as focused on the importance of the subject matter had I not taken decisive action in setting a clear foundation for working respectfully.

Instead, the message got out very quickly and we began a more defined journey toward instilling respect as a core value at Ryzex. We are not perfect but we are a lot better at working respectfully. Since working with character is a journey and not a destination, I know that we will never be done reinforcing the importance of respect and helping people apply this value every moment, every day. People at all levels in the company have to be relentless at observing, coaching, and acting on the behaviors underlying this value. Just the other day a situation came to my attention where a salesperson was yelling at an individual in shipping because we missed getting orders out on time and I've been at Ryzex for over six years…it requires consistent and constant commitment.

## (Self) Respect Starts Within

To be respectful is to be willing to see beyond our first impression[6].

As was the case with accountability, it is imperative to start by putting "self" in front of the word "respect." To consistently work and live this value, we need to be aware and understand what respect means. The root of the word RESPECT means to "look again.[7]" Literally, then, to be respectful is to be willing to see beyond our first and often superficial impression.

---

[6] www.leadershipcharacter.com/model.php (Accessed March 2011)
[7] Latin *respectus* from re + *spicere* to look, 14th century. www.merriam-webster.com/dictionary/respect (Accessed March 2011)

## We Mirror Each Other...Really

 Essentially we all have a need to belong, support each other, and contribute. This is not bologna and soft-headed mush; it's based on evolutionary science. One of the world's leading social economists, Jeremy Rifkin, author of *The Empathetic Civilization*, has captured powerful precepts on the concept of empathy.

Rifkin states, "Social scientists are beginning to reexamine human history from an empathic lens...The growing scientific evidence is that we are a fundamentally empathic species. This has profound and far-reaching consequences for society, and may well determine our fate as a species." And as a result it has implications for the workplace.

This is a pretty dense book to work through, but it is rich in insight. If you want a shortcut, I urge you to watch Rifkin's RSA eleven-minute video[8]. Rifkin refers to scientific data which shows that brain patterns mirror feelings in each other; not only amongst humans but between many of the animal kingdom.

My point in this underscores empathy as a key element within the respect framework of the Character Triangle. As people working together, a commitment to understanding what our teammates are feeling is progress. So at work: seek to understand and work from the belief that almost all of us want to belong and contribute. It's the civilized way to work together.

---

[8] http://www.youtube.com/watch?v=l7AWnfFRc7g (Accessed March 2011)

Respect requires us to be genuinely open to what the other person is really trying to communicate. What a powerful definition; **to be receptive** and **to look again.** So to be true to the root of respect, one has to continuously look at one's self again and again with openness and understanding. The point—we need to religiously examine the way we treat ourselves first and determine whether our coworkers would like to be treated the same way. Huh? Did I mean to state it that way? Yes, I sure did. If we treat ourselves with respect first, it is easier to be genuinely open to others and to treat them respectfully, too.

We all want to be listened to with understanding, treated with courtesy, and recognized for our contributions. If we continually put our "self" in front of the term "respect," we can usually step into another footsteps that much more easily and understand where that person is coming from. In a successful company, all must work together to succeed. With team members, we often do not take the time to openly "look again." Sometimes we are wary or even mistrustful of their intent. It is easy to become disappointed in others and most of us detest feeling duped or foolish. But, listening and looking again are in our control. It is not about what the other person does. It is about how we act and approach others.

### Who Should Get More Respect?
### Me, You, or that Ivy League Grad?

It was interesting that Elena Kagan, during the Senate Judiciary Hearings for appointment to the Supreme Court, toned down any hint of superior intellectualism (although she had a bit of a reputation for coming across that way). This Supreme Court nominee's best strategy seemed to be reflected in her down-to-earth humor as she quipped about, "...likely needing to get her hair done more often..." if successful in getting elected to the country's highest court.

Most of us don't like "uppity" condescending behavior regardless of how smart people are. We normally know when people are "smarter" and/or have superior credentials (like Kagan). But, the concept of respect is a matter of equality.

My point is that the value of respect, one of the core tenants of the Character Triangle, involves people treating each other with consistent decency regardless of differences, intellectual or otherwise. Let's face it; some people just are smarter than others. That's a fact. However we all expect to be treated at an interpersonal level with dignity regardless of I.Q. (You may recall how well the chairman of BP was received when he referred to Americans as the "little people" during the Louisiana Gulf oil crisis.) When I hire someone, I want to go to a restaurant and have dinner with them. How do they treat the wait staff? How do they treat the receptionist? How do they carry on a dinner conversation? Describing themselves in the third person is a bit of a concern, too. Any hint of superiority or arrogance, regardless of how great the resume is, and I pass.

Smart people who can get great results are sought after. Choose the same kind of people who get there by stepping on top of others? No thanks! And by the way it works both ways. Super-smart people with all the intellectual credentials shouldn't have to dumb it down. When it involves how we treat each other, it's not about smarts...it's about respect. We are all "Ivy League" when it comes to working together.

## So Respect is to be Earned, Right?

We often say respect is "earned," indicating—be it consciously or subconsciously—that others must prove themselves before "earning" our respect. Yet, if we really followed the principle of "looking again," perhaps respect for others would not come at the price of passing a subjective test to determine if they are worthy.

---

### Deafness Teaches Us to Listen

 Effective listening is a core foundation for treating each other with respect. Dame Evelyn Glennie is a deaf percussionist and highly accomplished musician. But her most powerful impact and legacy will likely be teaching us how to really listen. Her video[9] on www.ted.com is thirty-four minutes long but, as described by TED viewers, "jaw dropping."

Glennie teaches us to listen with our whole bodies and not to judge on the basis of shallow perception. Effectively listening to music (and people) requires us to FEEL the underlying vibrations. This involves patience, openness, and a genuine interest in receiving the melody and beat.

So, whether one enjoys Evelyn's music or not, the act of listening with depth and real sensitivity is a powerful lesson for us all. We need to pause and ask ourselves what is the underlying vibration and message? This means being present and concentrating on the dialogue. An exchange of words is only part of the communication.

In every interaction at work, it helps to ask more questions. Starting tomorrow, commit to genuinely asking for more understanding during every meeting or phone call. The more we model that behavior, the better listeners we become.

---

[9] http://www.youtube.com/watch?v=IU3V6zNER4g (Accessed March 2011)

Think of it this way: do we personally have to "earn" being listened to, treated courteously, and recognized for contributions? Really? We shouldn't. In this context, respect is not something to be earned but rather something to be given. **So to live with character is to give respect unconditionally to ourselves and others.** Think about the power and gratification of giving respect freely to all.

## Everything is a Process

Is there ever a time we shouldn't be listened to, treated with courtesy, and positively recognized? The logical answer to that is likely "no." So what might help us offer these elements of respect in an unconditional way at work? One important consideration is to understand that literally **everything is a process**.

When we accept the notion that **everything is a process,** it becomes easier to be open and understanding. If **everything is a process**[10], then everything can be viewed as a way or method of doing things. And we can confront the effectiveness of methods and ways without attacking each other personally. This is a subtle but an important principle for people in organizations to learn and apply. It helps us bridge the concepts of being performance and improvement driven, while still embracing the value of behaving respectfully. It is somewhat liberating to view the behavior of others as a process and to minimize judgment regarding intent. That is, no one is perfect; everything we or our coworkers do is a process. And if a process can be understood, it can be addressed and improved. It is respectful—and even necessary—to continuously improve our processes.

---

[10] Masaaki Imai, *Kaizen: The Key to Japan's Competitive Success*, McGraw-Hill Publishing Company, New York, 1986, pp. 17–21.

It is also reasonable and even necessary to positively confront unacceptable behavior when listening with understanding. However, relationships in the workplace often unravel when we attack each other verbally (or, in extreme cases, even physically) or question motives and character.

## Miscommunication Happens Often... and Is So Darned Hard

Earlier I referenced the remarkable percussionist Dame Evelyn Glennie. She teaches the importance and beauty in being ultra-sensitive to people's "vibrations." The following are some practical tools to help us connect with those vibrations when we have a miscommunication. I've drawn them from a *Harvard Business Review* blog[11] written by Peter Bregman, CEO of Bregman Partners, Inc.

"Who is responsible for making the first move to clear up a miscommunication?"

Peter's response, "Whoever sees it first."

I couldn't agree more. It is not about who is right or wrong or who makes the first move. It is about clearing up the misunderstanding. And as I stress so often, it's the self-accountable thing to do.

"How do we know that there is something deeper going on in a communication process?"

Peter's view is that "tone" is a clue. When the tone of the discussion has an edge to it, there is probably something not right. That may seem so obvious but how many times do we just run by that signal? My view is that this is a good time to really be present and try to take in those vibrations Evelyn talks about.

If the other person's response or view does not seem

[11] http://blogs.hbr.org/bregman/2010/07/how-to-avoid-and-quickly-recov.html (Accessed March 2011)

reasonable, especially when that person is normally reasonable, this is an alarm bell that something deeper is driving the response.

Bregman's advice: "Don't slam the other person for being unreasonable. And don't make the mistake of telling that person what they're really trying to say. Instead, even if you think you know what's going on, ask a question."

Holy cow...I couldn't agree more. And don't ask a patronizing or loaded question. First ask yourself what's going on and then genuinely ask the other person what is going on; you need to understand their feelings at a much deeper level.

The Respect value of the Character Triangle is based on listening and understanding. At work we come from such different angles and so much of our contact is remote. Fighting for understanding is the best for our teammates and the best for us, too. It is, however, hard work. It may be easier at the outset to ignore the miscommunication but it has a negative cumulative effect on our relationship. Be self-accountable; take the action to address it. Respect means asking a lot of questions for understanding. Bregman gives us a few good practical guides.

How often have you heard terms like "lazy," "jerk," and worse in conversations about others in the workplace? What's more, how often have each of us participated willingly in such conversations? It can be easy to lapse into a disrespectful attitude ourselves when the workplace environment tolerates, and in some cases even promotes it.

Therein lies the problem; even well-intended people can become disrespectful if the attitude is so pervasive that "everyone does it." And now more than ever, it is even easier to disrespect others behind their backs—and with multiple respondents. With email and social media tools we can forward, illustrate, and post hurtful comments online as well, often to large, widely distributed groups. Many of them are internal, some are external—all are harmful.

Remember the sales team having a poor quarter in the Be Accountable chapter? If the sales process is respectfully but rigorously examined, it is likely to be much more productive without adding emotionally charged comments such as, "Sales people are lazy and unmotivated," "Marketing sucks," etc.

Think of how many good, talented, creative, hardworking, passionate people organizations have lost over the years because they were disrespected, either verbally or simply by not being acknowledged for their passion and performance? This isn't just bad people skills; it's bad for business. The types of people who flourish in a disrespectful workplace are often the same individuals who spend more time blaming or disparaging others than looking inward to enhance their own performance. In almost every business, an organization's environment becomes much more constructive and productive when people agree to examine a process (BE RESPECTFUL) and approach the review from a "what, and how can I fix" attitude (BE ACCOUNTABLE).

## Listen with Understanding

Listening with understanding is hard work. One has to be present. We have to care what others are saying and meaning. Indeed, the idea that we have two ears and one mouth for a reason seems to be a little bit of a lost art. And yet, there can be no respect without active listening. It is enormously helpful and respectful when you work with someone who sincerely asks lots of questions for genuine understanding (as opposed to setting a trap to "get you," i.e. they know the answer before they ask the question).

When you genuinely open yourself to take another look to understand another individual, the respect value is significantly enhanced. Trust me; people know when you are really, actively listening versus just waiting for their mouth to stop moving so yours can start! Think about a time when your boss or coworker really cared and dug in to find out about your thoughts and actions. This became a golden opportunity for you to express yourself, openly and honestly, without fear of rebuke. What if he or she listened to understand the process and the thinking behind the application of it? Isn't that how you would like to be treated?

Listening does not always mean agreeing. In fact, Aristotle stated, "It is the mark of an educated mind to be able to entertain a thought without accepting it." In fact, highly respectful organizations are invigorated with constructive disagreement and conflict. A company full of "yes" men and women often means a company with no objective viewpoint, and one that is out of touch with the competition and customer.

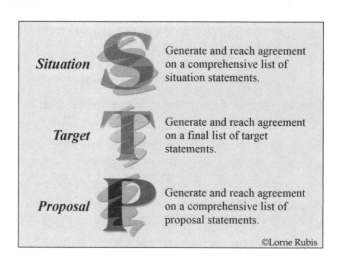

| | | |
|---|---|---|
| *Situation* | **S** | Generate and reach agreement on a comprehensive list of situation statements. |
| *Target* | **T** | Generate and reach agreement on a final list of target statements. |
| *Proposal* | **P** | Generate and reach agreement on a comprehensive list of proposal statements. |

©Lorne Rubis

Over the years I have used a simple tool to help my listening dialogue. It is called STP, Situation—Target—Proposal. It is timeless and yet so simple to apply. Refer to Appendix I for a more detailed description of the STP approach. And go to www.lornerubis.com to watch the STP video. The essence of STP is that if you work to understand the current environment **(Situation)** and objectives of others **(Target)**, then action-based dialog **(Proposal)** often has a successful outcome.

> **Note:** If using the STP model at work is your only take away from this book, you will have an immediate payback on your investment. Try it!

## Embrace Diversity

Diversity is a matter of benefiting from the unique angles of other people. Of course, when we capture the best combination of race, ethnicity, region, religion, culture, age, perspective etc., we demonstrate the sincerest application of respect. The richness of organizational diversity is directly related to how effective we are in listening and understanding the many viewpoints of others.

What benefit do we achieve if we have huge diversity in a population but miss the opportunity to listen to the rich perspective that comes from it? I learned this lesson as an eighteen-year-old student working on the railway as a section man. In case you are more accustomed to riding the rails than working them, a "section man" is one who does manual maintenance on the tracks.

My crew was populated by Portuguese, Poles, Ukrainians, Italians, Lebanese, and Yugoslavians. I was the most fluent in English, the lone university student, and younger than most of my coworkers by at least fifteen years. Very few could speak English well and most were very recent immigrants. They left their homelands for a "better life" and many abandoned better jobs back home for back-breaking railway work in a foreign land (Canada) as a matter of necessity.

I will be forever grateful that these men accepted a "kid" into their fold and were respectful enough to give me the chance to learn, often in very dangerous situations. I learned quickly that my command of the English language had zero correlation to intelligence. I also learned that cheese, fruit, homemade salami and whole grain bread (a typical European lunch), were a little more nutritious than my "American" bologna sandwich and a donut!

This was a basic lesson in the power of listening and understanding. I walked onto the job really thinking I was the smart guy. The greatest feeling in the world was when the boys invited me home for a glass of homemade wine. It was a statement that I had been recognized as a contributor and not just a summertime nuisance. The key point of this anecdote is that the general concept of accepting diversity is fundamental to respect. We cannot assume that we know it all based on our position and/or credentials. Learn from the unique angles of other individuals. Engage others to bring about the best results. Working together on a section crew that resembles the United Nations taught me these lessons early in my life and I will be always thankful to my rail yard mentors.

### Kindness is Free

 Tom Peters, one of the most important observers and writers on "excellence" in business, has a chapter with this title in his book *The Little Big Things: 163 Ways to Pursue Excellence.* Why? Kindness makes a huge difference to excellence in leadership. And I believe it is one of the key tenants of Respect.

He goes on to refer to a quote from Plato: "Be kind, for everyone is fighting a great battle." The point is that you and I need to look at things from the perspective of the other person. This means we have to care. That's hard work.

Kindness opportunities present themselves daily with teammates and others, including customers and suppliers. Being kind and thoughtful applies to almost every internal and external activity we're involved in. What a powerful currency kindness is, and it's totally free!

## Be Nice, Be Kind

Where have all the "nice" people gone? In conversation just the other day I overheard a comment that can basically be paraphrased as, "Being nice is a soft skill; my people need hard skills to survive in this business." Yes, we need to be tough-minded, make hard decisions, and act decisively, but I don't recall "tough" being synonymous with "mean."

In the organizations I have been involved in, I have found that the most admired people are usually the nicest as well. They genuinely treat people the same respectful way regardless of place, position, or stature, whether they

### Does Capitalism Allow for Kindheartedness?

Adam Phillips and Barbara Taylor in their recently published book *On Kindness* have released a short but thought-provoking treatise on the matter. They raise interesting questions. Is kindness for losers? Is kindness just narcissism in disguise? Does capitalism allow for kindheartedness? In conclusion, the authors argue that generosity of spirit and kindness is a more natural state of being. It does not need to be a forbidden pleasure. Indeed our attachments to others fulfill our sense of humanity.

My observations over the years, without the benefit of the psychoanalyst (Phillips) and historian (Taylor) is that kind (not naive) people are the winners in the most important sense of the word. My argument is that kindness is a key sub-element of respect.

The next time you need to work together with someone who is a little too stressed out, overextended (overworked?) or just plain tired, watch how much easier it is to have a more productive meeting when you extend this person additional kindness. We can succeed and thrive at work with kindness as a key part of who we are. In fact, the authors noted after considerable study—being kind is more natural and who we really are. It is okay to treat ourselves and others kindly. Really.

work in the corner office or on the front lines. They greet coworkers by name, acknowledge their presence, and normally smile and connect. They are literally never too busy to acknowledge and confirm. They are often the sincere example of politeness; opening doors, saying "please" and "thank you." Truly respectful people would not mindlessly think of leaving a mess for someone. They always clean up after themselves regardless of position. I am surprised and disappointed when executives leave their coffee cups and debris for others. It may be a small misstep in the grand scheme of things, but respectful people are nice people, plain and simple. Arrogance and respect do not go together. Being nice and being kind, while perhaps sounding mushy, is fundamental to acting with respect.

## Be Present

A colleague, we'll call him "Barry," told me an interesting story about his first meeting with a new CEO. Barry lived in a Blackberry culture, where everyone spent their time gazing down at email messages on their PDAs anytime, anywhere. Barry walked into the CEO's office for a first-time introduction and, just as the meeting began, the CEO's blackberry began violently buzzing on her desk.

Barry abruptly stopped and waited nervously for the boss to pick up the Blackberry. She looked Barry in the eye, deftly stashed the device in a desk drawer—out of sight and out of mind—and told him in no uncertain terms that he had her full attention. He was taken aback that she would make herself present **the way she did.**

How would you like to be treated in a similar situation? Respectful people always work hard to be physically and emotionally present when they interact with others. They have a commitment to be "in the now." This is another important attribute when it comes to respect. How thoughtfully do you give your undivided attention when working with your colleagues?

We often think we're too busy to be in the now, giving half of our attention, if that. But I've learned that when people come to you in a leadership position, it's rarely for insignificant reasons; giving them your time helps them help you, plain and simple.

---

### Sitting Quietly at Your Desk ...Shhh

Franz Kafka, widely recognized as one of the most important writers of the twentieth century, exclaimed the following: "You need not even leave the room. Remain sitting at your table and listen...simply wait, just learn to be quiet and still and solitary. The world will freely offer itself to you to be unmasked."

Of course Kafka and many other geniuses refer to this "stillness of the mind" as a route to opening up creativity. I believe it also is a foundation for respectful interaction between us as people and workmates. When I take time to quiet my mind and to be present, my listening skills and my presence increases significantly; more effective dialogue and problem solving often follows.

Having respectful interaction at work is vital for each of us to achieve a sense of value. When we are about to engage with others, let's allow ourselves that brief moment for the mind to go quiet in advance. Put everything else down; be present and listen. I guarantee the experience will be better for our teammates and us.

---

## Do You Know Someone Like Juanita?

"Juanita" is a finance manager at a major corporation and makes a point of greeting the receptionist with a pleasant and personal hello, and a smile of acknowledgement whenever she enters the office. Sometimes she brings a coworker a coffee and simply says thanks; she always remembers the receptionist's birthday with a small gift of appreciation.

She sincerely acknowledges the contribution made by people at all levels and in all positions. Juanita is a very direct person and a very good accountant. She is masterful in dealing with difficult issues in the organization. Coworkers have a high regard for Juanita, not just the work she does but the way she does it.

When you work with Juanita, very quickly you come to recognize that she is a great listener, always checking for understanding. She seems to intuitively facilitate a group to understand the situation, agree on targets, and fully explore proposals and actions. People like to work with Juanita because she is self-accountable and positively focused.

She really likes to get everyone's opinions on record before starting a new project and is committed to "moving the ball forward." She is known as a person who does not gossip or look to stir up organizational drama, recognizing this detracts from the reason she and her finance team are at work in the first place. When you meet Juanita or have a conversation with her, she makes you feel like you have her full attention.

## Do You Know Someone Like Geraldo?

"Geraldo" is very good as an assistant controller for his company. He gets his work done accurately, in a timely fashion, and protects the interests of the company well. Based merely on performance, Geraldo meets—even exceeds—the demands of his job description.

He is, however, very difficult to work with at times because people find him "moody." Depending on the day, or simply his mood, Geraldo will often not return a greeting to a team member, and is very personally critical of the management and colleagues. In Geraldo's opinion, most people are "not to be trusted."

He is thought to be a loner and doesn't like working in teams or attending meetings. He is famous for "tuning out" when in conversation, and is a master of the "sneer." Geraldo doesn't just think people are stupid; he has an actual list of the stupidest people in the company on his desktop.

Geraldo has very high standards for his fellow employees and those he considers worthy of his respect. He thinks that unless you have a CPA, you haven't earned a valued opinion. He detests salespeople and thinks they're spoiled whiners. He actually thinks that if everyone worked as hard as he did, and were as disciplined as the finance department, the company would be much better.

Both Juanita and Geraldo work for the same company and both are skilled accountants. Would the organization be better off with people who behaved more like Juanita or Geraldo? Both are very capable. However, one is wired to treat people with respect as defined above and the other (decidedly) less so.

We can argue that work should be performance—versus personality—based, but few of us work in a vacuum. (Come to think of it, do any of us?) Most of us are on, or lead, teams of very talented individuals who must work together for the betterment the company.

When teams can't communicate, interact, or perform without making derogatory or insensitive comments, then they can't live up to their potential. Having an employee who performs his/her job well but only in isolation detracts from the team's and, ultimately, the company's success.

And that's just in the short term. Over time, people who are on the negative side of the respect continuum restrict dialogue, open thinking and even build fear into the organization. At their worst, particularly in senior management positions, they become organization bullies. People do not want to incur their negative wrath and will behave in such a manner as to please these organizational bullies, often over the needs of the company or even the customer.

### Will You Have a Crucial Conversation Today?

 Being able to successfully navigate a crucial conversation is a vital skill for each of us to develop. Do we have a defined process and tools to do so?

A respected friend and leader introduced me to *Crucial Conversations*, written by Kerry Patterson, Joseph Grenny, Ron McMillan, and Al Switzler. The authors and I have learned the importance of being able to conduct a conversation when the stakes are high. As a CEO I can honestly state that the skillful ability of individuals and groups to conduct tough-minded, constructive dialogue is one of the distinguishing differences between failure and success. I believe when we have the right growth mindset, foundation values (The Character Triangle), and tools, we can literally talk about any issue with anyone and come to a better state of being. However we need the recipe and practice. As an example, the authors introduce the concept of **CRIB** to get past cross purposes. The **C** (commit to a mutual purpose); **R** (recognize the purpose behind the strategy); **I** (invent a mutual purpose); and **B** (brainstorm new strategies).

We are imperfect human beings and likely to fall outside the principles underlying the value of respect from time to time. But in order to live with true character, we must overwhelmingly believe in and display the underlying tenants. Be first. Be respectful.

This little tool set is just one of a number introduced in the book. The point is to recognize that having a successful crucial conversation is a learned process that requires understanding and purposeful practice. What process and tools do you use?

In order to fully embrace the value of RESPECT, I believe we have to be crucial conversation "certified." Becoming skillful at doing this will improve your contribution and relations in and out of work. Invest in being able to conduct a crucial conversation. (Note: there are other solid processes and tools in addition to those offered by Vitalsmarts[12]. I have no commercial arrangement with them but they come highly endorsed.)

---

[12] http://www.vitalsmarts.com/ (Accessed March 7, 2011)

 **The BE Respectful Playbook**

Tear a page out of the Respect Playbook and keep the following respectful principles in mind while working with Character.

**1.0 Start with "self" first and "look again."** Take the time to reassess and reevaluate every situation from an "inside out" perspective by putting the "self" before "respect." Take the time to look again with openness and receptivity.

**2.0 Remember that everything is a process and all processes can be improved.** A process is distinct from the person.

**3.0 Always examine the process, behavior, and situation first; never attack a person.** Remember, open dialogue and discussion—even disagreement—does not equal personal attacks and petty sniping.

**4.0 Treat yourself the way you want others to be treated; then do it.** Be nice. One can be very tough-minded and results-driven, and still be courteous and accessible to all others. Arrogance provides no value.

**5.0 Listen with understanding[13]; be present and look at every perspective**. Diverse angles and great dialogue are fundamental to being respectful. Give others your full attention when interacting.

**6.0 Use the STP process (See Appendix for more) as a great listening tool, problem-solving process, and a way to get people aligned.**

---

[13] http://www.ehow.com/how_2307229_listen-understanding.html (Accessed March 8, 2011)

## Whose View is Right?!

Understand that every world view, including yours and including mine, has limitations. Listen, learn, be humble... be respectful.

The tragic mass shooting in Tucson on January 8, 2011, raised the issue of intolerance and acceptance of diverse viewpoints, including but not limited to the provocative and potentially dangerous aspects of name calling and labeling. Unfortunately we have people with very public platforms making a living out of intolerance rather than promoting dialogue and understanding. They often argue that THEIR world view is not only the right way but that it's the only way.

Cindy Wrigglesworth, the founder and CEO of www.deepchange.com, has done important work on **Spiritual Intelligence**, which she describes as the ability to act with Wisdom and Compassion while maintaining equanimity (inner and outer peace), regardless of the circumstances.

She and her organization measure twenty-one attributes that they believe capture progress on the spiritual leadership continuum. Just ONE measurement area of spiritual intelligence is around the notion of world-view; the way one sees the world. A well-developed mindset regarding this world-view, according to the people at Deep Change, is, "Everyone has a world-view and that every world-view has limitations. This keeps us humble and open to learning. We genuinely value other people's perspective."

The RESPECT value as defined in the Character Triangle fully embraces the critical importance of valuing other people's perspectives. The elements of respect as I define it overlap with many of the dimensions that

Wrigglesworth and her team believe leads to greater spiritual intelligence.

The workplace is often filled with a "my way or the highway" perspective. This is especially dangerous when authority is attached to intolerance. Of course there are rules and policies that need following. Chaos and anarchy aren't very practical. However the ability to really value other people's perspectives is vital to a respectful and healthy organization culture.

Take an honest look at where you may not be genuinely valuing another person's perspective at work. Is there anywhere that you are intolerant? Why? What might you learn if you open up to better understand the other view? Remember that every world view has its limitations. Be respectful.

## Practice the Plays

Now that you've studied the Playbook, here is an opportunity to practice the plays themselves. Take the following actions and journal them below:

↙ Take stock of your thoughts and actions for one week. How do you talk to and treat yourself? Do you treat all people the way you would like to be treated?

_____

_____

_____

_____

_____

↙ Identify people who effectively display the principles as described above. How effective are they as organization leaders/influencers?

_____

_____

_____

_____

_____

↙ Who are the biggest violators of these principles? Watch how people interact with these people.

_____

_____

_____

_____

_____

↙ Practice using the STP tool wherever you can. See what happens when people develop a common understanding of the situation and targets. Do acceptable proposals/ actions evolve more effectively?

_____

_____

_____

_____

_____

↙ Try to give people your undivided attention in any conversation you participate in for a week. Do you notice any differences?

_____

_____

_____

_____

_____

✔ Are you applying the respect principles personally first? Or do you find yourself attacking the person...you? It is difficult to be respectful to others in the full sense of the word without being respectful to yourself first? Look again.

_____

_____

_____

_____

_____

✔ Identify five situations where you practiced the principles of respect as described in this chapter.

_____

_____

_____

_____

_____

✔ What worked? What did you learn?

_____

_____

_____

_____

_____

## Personal Learning on Being Respectful

In Chapter 1, I talked about how I started my adult working life as a twenty-one-year-old teacher at a junior high school. The thing about middle school kids is that they thrive on the value of respect; they give and withhold it, often in cruel ways. Teaching at St. Nicks was one of the greatest experiences of my life. I found out that if I genuinely cared and treated these kids with respect, they would knock themselves out to reciprocate.

Of course, it would be simplistic of me to reflect back and to determine that my successful experience at the school was exclusively related to the value of respect. I had a belief that every kid could be successful and contribute. Not everyone at St. Nicks could be an "A" student or great athlete, but everyone—everyone—had something to contribute. I was admittedly demanding and laid out high expectations of conduct, but these kids always responded. We listened to each other and cared for each other. This was when I began to understand my future mantra that **everything is a process.**

Attacking a person is useless, but coaching a person to apply a process more effectively is a powerful tool. Even "attitude," which thirteen-year-olds are famous for, can usually be constructively addressed by listening, being present and examining the process rather than attacking the person. Many things happened over my four years at that school as it dramatically improved academically and athletically. Everyone began to feel like "winners." One important element to the transformation was a basic ethos of respect that emerged as a genuine part of the school's character.

Fast forward several years—and careers—later: I was a negotiator for a construction organization and the primary contract was with a major building trade union. The business manager of the union was a classical "tough union guy." I was a little apprehensive going to the bargaining table with the guy based on his reputation. He could "get into your kitchen," as they say, and intimidation was a conscious strategy he regularly employed.

Working with this guy was challenging, to say the least. In the end, he was about respect. The more I listened, however unreasonable some arguments appeared to be on the surface, the better we were able to determine the principles underneath the union's request. If I didn't "look again," I might have followed the footsteps to an impasse, which was the historical outcome most negotiators encountered when dealing with this guy. In the end, it was a two-way street. The more we listened to each other, working on the process rather than making it personal, the better we did.

Again, I don't want to over-simplify the progress and positive outcome in this situation exclusively to the value of respect. However, in this and countless experiences in my forty-plus years of working, the best things I've been a part of have been accomplished when people have treated each other with respect based on the above principles.

## Donuts and the Thought in the Middle

 As CEO, I'm on most of the company's email groups for better or worse. Sometimes I get the mundane… announcements of lost car keys, etc. However I keep an eye on one kind of mundane email usually entitled "Cakes!"

This is the email "shout out" in our office in the United Kingdom (UK office) that pastries are available for all. Something or someone is being celebrated. Interestingly, the "morale" score in the UK has climbed with the frequency of the "CAKES!" emails.

Why? I don't know the exact science or statistical significance but I do know that celebration and generosity of spirit impact company morale in very positive ways. The more celebrations and hoopla the better.

My dad was in palliative care for about four months before he died. On one of my last days on the floor with my dad, I brought in two dozen donuts and thanked the nursing staff for their ongoing, loving care. These health practitioners want two-dozen carbohydrate loaded "sugar bombs" as much as a flat tire. But they cheered and were grateful. The bigger issue relates to the acknowledgment, thank you, and respect that comes from thinking of others and in sharing. It is not the donut but the thought in the middle. It sounds silly and maybe even trite; it's not.

Cakes! Donuts! … a little fuel for respect. Bring some in today!

When people get into positions of authority in a hierarchy, I often wonder why arrogance related to position grows out of proportion. What happens when they start to believe that everyone else below them has to earn their respect and that they get to give it out to those who deserve it?

This "big shot" thinking is disrespectful and will inevitably be counterproductive. When I meet other leaders in other organizations, I can learn a lot in a quick walk around with them through their organization. It is help to observe:

- ✔ How do they greet people and vice versa?

- ✔ Are people open or fearful?

- ✔ Does the leader say "please" and "thank you"?

- ✔ Does he know people's names?

- ✔ How does she describe others?

I had a colleague I worked with at US WEST who used to call people "nothingburgers" with disdain. I was one of seven people reporting to Dick McCormick, who was chairman and CEO of this Fortune 50 Company at that time. I remember having dinner with this very talented woman, and she started describing the executive team with contempt and personal descriptions that were unflattering at best.

I remember thinking that if she said this about the executives, how would she be as a leader who could inspire open, constructive, respectful dialogue? She was perceptive in outlining why the organization needed to become more nimble, and she was a change agent; but why the personal attacks? I remember telling Dick that if she were to be promoted to an executive position, which she eventually was, that he and others needed to discuss this behavior with her. When she abruptly left US WEST, the rumor is that people put "Ding Dong! The Witch is Dead" on the phone system; not exactly respectful in its own right, but an example of how people felt about being treated with disdain during her "reign."

---

### Doing to Others IS Doing to Ourselves

I think it is important to consider the premise that the way we treat others is likely an indication of how we treat ourselves. As an example, if we are mean to others we can put ourselves in a foul mood. When we are uncaring or indifferent we can become empty inside. Leo Babuata at www.zenhabits.com describes[14] this very thoughtfully.

The essence of respect stems from being present and mindful of every interaction with every human being. It starts with the simple things. How about just recognizing that when we go through a door, there might be someone behind us, instead of letting it "slam." Perhaps that is a metaphor, keeping the door open for every person we interact with.

Kindness and presence takes practice. But when we act this way to others, I genuinely feel that we treat ourselves similarly and the good will becomes reinforcing.

The work environment is a fertile place for acting with respect. If we are mindful of every interaction with colleagues and customers and recognize that we are doing to ourselves... well, the outcome can be powerfully positive. Now how do you want to respond to that email?

---

I have had the experience of working closely with billionaires, and with people whose net worth was just

---

[14] http://zenhabits.net/kindfully/ (Accessed March 2011)

slightly under the "B" word. I took notice of those who were thoughtful about treating people in their workplace respectfully. When Mr. and Mrs. Anschutz came into L.A. and the Great Western Forum, they were the first to say "Hello" to all members of the staff. They went out of their way to be open and accessible. The Roski's, Anschutz's partners and co-owners of the Kings Hockey club, were the same way. I worked for Kirby McDonald, another highly successful businessman in the same genre, and he is one of the most fun-loving nice guys you could spend time with. These people are obviously tough-minded business people and have, like all of us, their own shortcomings. However, I have always believed that their exceptional listening skills, ability to be totally present during interactions, and genuine "niceness" contributed to their success. They embodied respect in all interactions I had with them. (Note: Stories about Steve Jobs, CEO and Apple founder; and Larry Ellison, CEO and founder of Oracle; treating others in questionable ways are legendary and public. So I am not naively arguing that treating others with respect is a unilateral correlation with business success. At the same time these guys are smart enough to have surrounded themselves with many people who do promote a culture of respect.)

If respect could use a spruce up where you work, remember to start with YOU first, and establish a process that can bring about the results you want. Start acting on it today (See Be Accountable chapter).

> *"If we lose love and self respect for each other, this is how we finally die."*
>
> — Maya Angelou

# CHAPTER 4

## BE Abundant

Abundance

©Lorne Rubis

## Give up your Mitts!

 I like to tell a story of my dad's time in the palliative care unit shortly before he died. My mom got a call from a friend of my dad who was in her late eighties. She insisted on visiting my dad in the hospital "to say goodbye before he dies." So she talked her nurse into driving some sixty miles in the dead of a Western Canadian winter so she could get to his bedside. Why?

Apparently some eighty-some years ago my dad and his neighbor friend Alice, the lovely gal referred to above, had to walk three miles to and from school. One miserable blizzard, with frigid temperatures below -30 degrees, found my dad and Alice struggling to walk home. Alice said her hands were so cold she was weeping in pain. Her mittens got wet sitting on the classroom radiator and froze along with her hands on the trek home. My dad, seven years old at the time, gave Alice his mittens to wear instead. She never forgot that generosity.

Be abundant. Give up your mitts. You may get a hug eighty years later. Your generosity matters.

Dick McCormick was the chairman and CEO of US WEST (you may recall Dick from the previous chapter). It was my first day reporting to him, one of seven executives that did so regularly, and I remember sitting in his office. Dick was a lanky Midwesterner who had this certain Irish twinkle in his eyes and an easy laugh to match. He was also one of the best observers of people I have ever encountered, a personal trait that is often under-appreciated as a vital business tool.

During that first meeting, Dick pulled over a tripod with

chart paper on it and scratched out the three things he wanted me to focus on in the company. One of the points was to help Chuck Lillis, at that time senior VP of Marketing, with what Dick semi-humorously referred to as "the vision thing."

I was excited by the prospect, but immediately concerned. Not only was this my first assignment, and one I certainly wanted to excel at, but I was basically being asked to step into another executive's wheelhouse and tinker with his progress to date.

I mean, how would Chuck respond if I got involved in his arena? My sense of foreboding proved unfounded. Chuck, rather than seeing this intrusion from a perspective steeped in scarcity, instead embraced me as a resource that could really add to the overall organization. Even though I reported to the CEO, Chuck did what he was famous for; he deputized me into his camp.

With his sponsorship, I became the facilitator of a new strategic process that was eventually dubbed, the "Cottage Strategy." By most people's analysis, the work completed through this process went on to have a profoundly positive impact on the company as well as its shareholders.

In the fall of 2009, some fifteen years AFTER the Cottage Strategy started driving big changes at US WEST, Chuck and I were together at a University of Oregon event that Chuck and his wonderful wife Gwen were hosting. It was very personally rewarding to hear Chuck describe the value and results of the Cottage Strategy process to the many dignitaries at this event. The spinout of US WEST into two entities and the eventual strategic sale of one to AT&T and the other to Qwest are legendary in terms of financial results for US WEST shareholders: a classic "home run."

### Seth Godin Gets It!

 Are you a Linchpin? *Linchpins, Supporters and Leeches* author and marketing guru Seth Godin describes these categories of people. I strongly urge you to read his recently published book, *Linchpin*.

The people in the "leech" category are those Godin describes as pessimists and obstructionists. Godin states they are "driven by fear, they set out to slow you down, whittle you down, and average you down." This is the antithesis of being "abundant."

The third element of the Character Triangle is being Abundant. This means being generous of spirit and an optimist. It also embodies a deep belief in a successful outcome. Put an emphasis on the importance of being generous of spirit.

Think about the people that make an incredible impact—they give! As Godin states, "The economy has been better and worse. Through it all the market seeks out, recognizes, and embraces artists, people we can't live without."

Godin's type of "artist" has nothing to do with fine arts, but instead, being able to make a difference and contribute value to one's craft, regardless of whether or not it's in the board room or fixing kitchen sinks.

Be abundant. Be generous. Be an "artist." Give everything you have to have an impact.

Many other fortuitous events contributed to US WEST's positive strategic outcome, of course, but if it wouldn't have been for the Cottage Strategy and subsequent execution of its principles by Dick, Chuck, and other executives, there may not have been the two separate companies. It created a way for US WEST to value the true worth of the company's unique and distinct assets. It's easy to tally the numbers and consider the above story a success, but if you track back to the beginning with key players acting *without* character, the story could have had a very different ending.

If Dick, Chuck, or any number of players throughout the growth of the Cottage Strategy, had shared a different attitude, I might not be writing this today. If Chuck hadn't trusted a new executive (me), and hadn't welcomed me as a contributor, the ending might have changed drastically. Either way, the attitude of the leaders at US WEST had everything to do with the opportunity I was given, and the success they later enjoyed. Fortunately, theirs was an attitude of abundance.

## It's All About the Attitude: Abundance Versus Scarcity

My experience is that people tend to lean either toward a philosophy of **abundance** or a philosophy of **scarcity**. What's the difference? Well, as you might have guessed by now, it's all about attitude connected to behavior that validates a way of thinking.

Abundance-oriented people seem to approach work and life in general as if they were **meant to be prosperous**. The wonderful thing about these people is that they see the objective of life as development and growth. Even better, when they can't actually touch, see or feel them, abundance-oriented people believe the resources for their success are available—somewhere.

Abundant people do not have to take anything away from anyone else to be successful. They believe that it is a divine right for every person to create, advance, and grow, and not to impede others with that growth.

Don't get me wrong, abundance-oriented people live within the same resource constraints that scarcity-thinking people do; they can't just "wish it" and make more resources appear. However, abundance-oriented people don't allow a lack of resources to be the reason why they can't find a way to move their situation to a more desirable state. Going back to self-accountability, if they don't have what they need, abundance-oriented people ask and answer what and how they need to do, get, and be where they want to be.

It is literally fun to work beside—or with—someone who is abundance-focused. They are competitive but, rather than being out to beat someone, the essence of their competitive drive is to advance something; for themselves, for teammates, coworkers, colleagues—for all involved. In fact, abundance-oriented people relish other people's success and achievements. They never feel the need to diminish what other people have done, or feel threatened when others succeed. They see other coworkers' accomplishments as great examples of what is possible, and often internalize what other people did to succeed, as guidelines for their own success.

Such people see abundance everywhere, and not just in mere things. A coworker's positivity, or resourcefulness, a life lesson, a strategy, an example, a formula, all are seen as tools to become more abundant.

If you have ever been on a high-performing team in work, sports, the arts, etc., you know how the desire to advance is exhilarating. Great teams find a way to acknowledge the contribution of all members (respect) and all members seem to have the ability to ask *what* and *how* they can contribute (self-accountable) to the collective abundance. (And, of course, they take positive action in that regard.)

# Coach John Wooden—Character Hall of Fame

*"Never try to be better than anyone else...but always try to be the best you can be."*

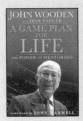 This was the fatherly advice given to the legendary college basketball coach John Wooden, who passed away on June 4, 2010, at the age of ninety-nine. The great thing about John Wooden is that he was revered more for the man he was than for being college's best basketball coach ever.

While his fame can be attributed to the remarkable championship run, coaching the UCLA Bruins hoop team, my belief is that Wooden would have stood above the crowd regardless of the size of his platform. Much has been written about Coach Wooden and I encourage you to spend some time learning more about his character. I really enjoyed the audio interview conducted by Anthony Robbins, called *Power Talk*.[15] While talking to Robbins, Coach Wooden emphatically noted that from very early in life, he learned to focus on what he could control: his own behavior. By doing this, Coach looked at every minute of every day as an opportunity to contribute, and did not waste time concerning himself with what he could not control. This is core to self-accountability. But with Wooden one could also easily expound on his living and breathing respect and abundance, too. He was truly a man with character and another member of the Character Hall of Fame[16].

---

[15] Anthony Robbins and Paul Zane Pilzer. *Powertalk!* ZCI Publishing, Dallas, TX, 1994.

[16] For more on the Character Hall of Fame, go to http://www.lornerubis.com/character-hall-of-fame/.

> ## Gold Medal with Character
>
> Jim Abbott had a great career as a baseball pitcher. He pitched the gold medal winning game for Team USA at the 1988 Summer Olympic Games. He also pitched a no-hitter as a New York Yankee. These are noteworthy feats in their own right. Jim accomplished these milestones without the use of his right hand, a "handicap" he was born with.
>
> But Jim never saw the "lack" of anything in his life. He grew up with the belief that he could accomplish what most able bodies did; and even more. He also received and accepted support along the way. Jim tells the story about his Grade 2 teacher who spent an entire weekend learning to tie his own shoes with his right hand tied behind his back, so he could teach Jim how to do it one handed on Monday. A seven-year-old aspiring baseball player translated that care into self accountable action, and the generosity of this teacher (and many other supporters) lives forever through Jim.
>
> Be generous—be abundant. We might inspire someone to win a gold medal against all odds. Plus we all win the gold medal of living with character. Jim Abbott (and by extension his Grade 2 teacher) is in our Character Hall of Fame.[17]

My experience is that abundant people are often rich in character because they have the ability to overcome adversity and uncertainty; knowing that success is a matter of perseverance based on the journey of development and contribution only increases their abundance.

The popular philosopher Eckhart Tolle states in his 2005 book *A New Earth, Awakening to Your Life's Purpose*, that **who you think you are** is intimately connected to **how you**

---

[17] Ibid.

**see yourself treated by others.** I really believe in Tolle's proposition that, "If all you see is 'lack,' that is likely what you will get."

Tolle also writes, "Some people believe that they have nothing to give and that the world or other people are withholding from them what they need."

He goes on to powerfully state, "If the thought of lack—whether it be money, recognition or love—has become part of who you think you are, you will always experience lack."

How many of us experience negative self-talk throughout the day that feeds into this notion that "lack" is a part of who we are? How different our lives could be if we gradually begin to pepper such self-talk with the acknowledgement that life is full of the resources we need. When we acknowledge that what we have and need is available, and that we have much good in our life, we quickly realize that the foundation for being abundant is already there.

My experience is that abundant people really work from that perspective; it isn't necessarily that they're "naturally positive or happy," but that they have purposefully cultivated an attitude of positivity that has increased their happiness.

Of course they have days that feel "lousy" and, as the bumper sticker aptly states, "Shit happens." The great thing is that abundance and scarcity are more inner states than outer conditions. Remember, it's all about the attitude connected to our actions. We truly do have the power to think about abundance as a state of mind.

## Abundance as a State of Mind

At the age of fifty, I decided to leave my COO position at Zones to join a voiceover Internet protocol (VOIP) startup. It was 2000 and I was sure that my due diligence in joining this

## Smile or Die

*I believe that positive optimism is important in a workplace.*

 Optimism is connected to the value of abundance in the sense that one focuses more on the "have" than "have not." On the other hand I don't promote nor believe in blind optimism. Sometimes things are just plain difficult, painful, and lousy. We get hurt, feel bad, and frankly can mistreat or be mistreated by others. These are facts and part of the human condition. How we respond though is often in our control and a choice we can willingly make. Being abundant is the choice to move forward, which often appropriately involves getting help from others. Acclaimed journalist, author, and political activist, Barbara Ehrenreich, provides a measure of balance in acting/thinking realistically while remaining positive[18].

In the workplace we need both: tough-minded realism on the status of things; and positive, forward movement in response. They are not mutually exclusive. One thing you can do is to insist on providing and asking for data in reviewing job-related matters. Facts keep blind positive thinking and helpless despair in check.

breakthrough technology opportunity would pay off. Based on the analysis of many trusted advisors, the new company was a "can't lose" business (this was before SKYPE). After all, it combined great technology marketed as superb customer value, along with the best and brightest people, underwritten

[18] http://www.youtube.com/watch?v=u5um8QWWRvo&feature=email (Accessed March 2011)

by top-line Silicon Valley venture money. By everyone's account, it was going to be a "big hit"—maybe even a home run as noted in the US WEST story.

Of course in 2001, this startup—along with many other good (and poor) ventures—crashed and burned. This was a horrible time in my life for something like this to happen— kids in high school and college, and looking at starting over at fifty years old…*hmmm*, not good.

Yet despite the grim circumstances, I genuinely believed that something would come along after the crash—and it did. And it's not the only time; I had a basis for my belief that "something would come along." Throughout my life, in fact, the deep belief that the resources were available for me to make a contribution has been unfailing.

**In essence, it becomes a "chicken or the egg" type relationship. Did something come along because I believed it would, or did my strong belief in abundance help me will it into being?**

I do not embrace or follow all the aspects of the "law of attraction"[19] but I do believe abundance is a state of mind and it contributes materially to attracting the resources you need to get things done. This doesn't mean things come easy, or that life is without worry. And having strong beliefs and actions based on self-accountability and respect are brother and sister to being abundant.

I believe that we have a God-given right to health, peace of mind, and wealth. This is abundant thinking. And if one or more of these factors is missing, we have the right to believe that it is only a matter of time before we achieve a better state.

---

[19] The Law of Attraction, as popularized in the book *The Secret* by Rhonda Byrne.

Of course, as self-accountable people, we are taking *what* and *how* action to propel us forward. I do not want to foolishly or naively minimize the difficulties that most of us will face in any one of these three categories during life's journey.

Starting over in the business world at fifty was far from easy, and didn't happen overnight. Were there anxious mornings, worrisome days, and sleepless nights? Certainly. But, each was tempered with belief in myself and belief in the abundant blessings of my life. And sometimes things do happen that are beyond our control that can make the climb out of a tough situation very steep. Working from the premise that we have resources available to us to change things for the better is the best way to constructively view the world we work and live in.

Abundant-thinking people are prepared to live in the world of uncertainty. They take calculated risks because they have faith that things **will work out for the better.** They believe, often unfailingly, that you cannot succeed with an attitude of doubt and unwarranted anxiety (fear).

Abundant people recognize that even success is in a constant state of flux, and to arrive at a plateau is the platform for a new beginning. Change brings growth, and growth brings success; and all are part of the abundance process. Although they expect success for themselves, abundant people know that there could be setbacks and they rebound from failure with newfound learning and enthusiasm. This is not blind naiveté in the ways of the world, but pure belief in the power of positive results. It is not unrealistic positive thinking, but (so much) more than that. It is *abundant* thinking.

Jealousy and negativity are a part of daily work life. But think about that for a moment. Seriously reflect on it: what good is ever derived from acting with jealousy or negativity towards anyone? If you find that someone is getting more recognition than you, although you believe that you deserve at least as much, how do you react? What do you do?

Contrary to what your ego may be whispering over your shoulder, abundant people applaud the recognition others receive. They generally believe that another person's success does not detract from what they are doing. In fact, it reinforces their belief that abundance is present—and available to all.

Abundance does not exist in a vacuum (or the mind alone), nor can it flourish without taking action. The best way to reinforce abundance is to be the most generous, giving person you can be at work (and in all aspects of life). This means sincerely giving of oneself without expecting payback. This doesn't mean we shouldn't be shrewd in commercial dealings. It's not about being taken advantage of, but helping others succeed. That's because abundant people are open to sharing what makes them successful.

Abundant-behaving people are often the first to help out a colleague or rookie coworker. They are not afraid of giving away their "secret sauce" fearing that someone may take something away from them. After all, they believe in expanding and abundant resources. My experience in the work world is that those who are the biggest, most sincere givers are most often the biggest receivers.

So in the spirit of self-accountability and abundance, what if we all staked out a better state of being and asked *what* and *how* we might do to make it that way? What if we believed more strongly in our ability to make a positive difference? What if we respectfully engaged in dialogue with others to begin that forward progress?

Remember that working with character is evidenced by, and built upon, the guiding principles of being accountable, respectful, and abundant. Sometimes our work environment

### $5 a Day

Harvard did a study that affirmed that spending five dollars a day on others increased people's sense of self and well-being. You can also refer to a study by University of British Columbia psychologist Elizabeth Dunn.[20] The overall message here of course is that giving is one of the most powerful elements in creating positive well-being.

So why do we have such difficulty with this in the work context? We do not literally have to spend five dollars on people at work, but we can generate positive well-being by giving in small, yet meaningful, ways. One of these ways is to give encouragement and recognition. When we take the time to observe and acknowledge other people in a positive way, everybody wins.

Tom Peters suggests in his book *The Little Big Things: 163 Ways to Pursue Excellence* that the positive to negative ratio might be out of balance at work, "A lot of managers have the hardest time giving any positive reinforcement." So how about you and I commit to spending "five dollars" on each other at work EVERY DAY by recognizing one another in a genuine way. The Return on Investment is fast and bigger than we may realize.

is a poor match with these principles. Should we suffer in silence, or take action? In this case we have a right, and even an obligation, to find a better match. We have a given amount of time to make a contribution in the workplace. Where are

[20] http://www.publicaffairs.ubc.ca/2010/02/08/happiness-under-a-microscope-ubc-helps-lead-a-new-scholarly-focus-on-wellbeing/ (Accessed March 2011)

[21] 2080 hours/year (the number of standard work hours in a typical business year) for forty-seven years (starting at age eighteen and working to retirement at age sixty-five) equals 74,760 total hours worked in a typical lifetime.

you in the time/work continuum?[21] We should expect to be able to live and work in an environment that reinforces the value set we can flourish in, and not consistently "swim upstream" just to do the right thing.

Every organization, being made up of processes or a lack of processes, is run by humans with all degrees of strengths and shortcomings. Sometimes the match just isn't there and we have a responsibility to move on and seek—as well as spread—our abundance elsewhere. Out of respect for those around us, it is important to find a way to contribute—or leave.

## Do You Know Someone Like Fatimah?

Fatimah is one of those people who seem to be generous as a way of life. She is a technician at a top company who sees the greatness in doing high quality work, whether she is recognized for it or not. (She makes herself a *Linchpin* as Seth Godin describes it by the book of the same name). When new team members are hired, she is always enthusiastic about the assets they bring to the organization and the first to volunteer to "show them the ropes."

Fatimah likes to share best practices and is always looking for better ways to do her job, although she's an industry pro and long-time veteran. Fatimah is resistant to back-biting and gossiping and has respectfully discouraged it in her department and elsewhere.

Although she recognizes the value in standard operating procedure, Fatima is very forthcoming about ways she thinks she can improve the flow of material through her bench. When tools and test equipment started disappearing from her work area recently, Fatimah came up with several ideas about how she, as a technician, could minimize this from happening.

Fatimah makes it a matter of character to continuously improve. She believes that the more she invests in herself and others, the more valuable she will be as a technician and coworker. Like everyone, Fatimah has good days and not-so-good days, but sees her life at work as a vehicle for growth, development, and contribution.

## Do You Know Someone Like Raj?

Raj is very concerned about his job as a technician at a Fortune 500 company. The service business for data equipment may be going away. His approach to keeping his job as long as possible is to make himself less expendable than the other techs. As far as he is concerned, it's "every man for himself." There is no way he is going to help the "newbies" get adjusted to their jobs. What? So they can become competition?

"They can learn the hard way," just like he had to. Why help someone take your job? There are only so many jobs to go around to begin with, and his first priority is to feed his family. This "team stuff" is a bunch of bunk and management propaganda, according to Raj. There is only a certain amount to go around in any place and Raj is going to get his share.

Someone once told Raj that "information is power," and he believes that firmly. He also believes the only way to maintain power is to use it over others. He is going to be valuable because no one is going to know how to fix a certain gear but him. Raj makes a point of downplaying the high quality scores of other techs. They usually get better parts, easier devices to work on; and, for some reason, his supervisors seem to be easier on them. A lot of them,

---

### The Life You Can Save

Philosopher Peter Singer is the author of *The Life You Can Save*. Dan Heath and others helped create a three-minute video[22] that introduces Singer's thinking on the topic. I encourage you to watch it reference to thinking with abundance.

Now what if we took the same concept as captured in the video and applied it to our personal situation at work? I apologize for comparing saving lives of the poor in the same ballpark as most of our business situations. Of course these comparisons are on completely different moral planes. However the concept I want to stress is to not become overwhelmed by the big numbers or the daunting size of the task. When we think about the magnitude of the "end game" we can feel that we just don't have enough to get it done. We "throw in the towel" and focus on the lack of resources. Yet sometimes five percent of extra effort here and there adds up to a wave of change. This abundant thinking can often lead to real and sustainable improved results.

When we think we have enough to start; it can lead to finding enough to finish. If you want something to be better or different at work find that first five percent and go from there. We have enough to start. It is acting with abundance.

---

according to Raj, are management "brown-nosers."

Believe it or not, Fatimah and Raj work in the same company. Clearly, there is a fundamental difference in their approach to character, let alone abundance. Where would you rather work? A shop full of people like Fatimah? Or a company full of people like Raj?

---

[22] http://www.youtube.com/watch?v=onsIdBanynY (Accessed March 2011)

Purely from a skill perspective, Fatimah and Raj are both good technicians, but their values result in major differences in behavior. Fatimah is always looking forward and expanding, while Raj is looking over his shoulder and hoarding. Fatimah expects to grow and contribute. Raj expects to be the last tech standing.

Think of the question more personally: who would you want on your team, Fatimah or Raj? An organization full of abundance-thinking people pulls everyone forward. The atmosphere sparkles with generosity and optimism. The belief, the behavior, the focus—these become a constantly evolving, more desired state of being.

## Stage Right: You and Me

Tom Peters relays an interesting story in his book *The Little Big Things: 163 Ways to Pursue Excellence*. He tells of a situation where a professor was presenting from the bottom of a bowl-like classroom. Without this teacher knowing, the students were instructed by an organization psychologist conducting an experiment, to nod (noticeably but not in unison) when the professor moved stage right. And, not to nod when he was in the center or stage left during his lecture. As the story goes, the professor was soon pasted to the corner of stage right and stayed there most of the class. Peter's point: such is the power of deliberate positive reinforcement.

Encouragement and positive recognition usually help people move forward. You and I can do that right now. We don't have to have a certain title, minimum salary grade, or academic certificate to spread it out genuinely and freely. Offering a "Thanks" or "Nice job" is so easy. We don't have to be over the top. Even a smile, small pin, five-dollar Starbucks gift card, or a shoulder hug counts. Be a leader and offer it up. Be self-accountable to be abundant. Okay, now...everybody... move someone to stage right!

 **The BE Abundant Playbook**

Here is the third page of your Character Triangle Playbook, for being Abundant. After this, your Playbook will be complete, and you will have tools to better apply all elements of the Character Triangle and to step forward with Character. Remember, these are habitual behaviors so they will take some time to fully embrace and apply consistently. It takes continual practice.

1.0 **Be self-abundant in thinking.** Being abundant is a state of mind. Be self-abundant first. If you see yourself as prosperous, you will be focused on becoming prosperous. If you see yourself as lacking, you will focus on all that you lack. Remember that we have to be self-abundant first.

2.0 **Act with abundance; take calculated risks.** Embrace the deeply held belief that things will work out for the best and that you have right to material wealth, peace of mind, and health.

3.0 **Avoid negative people and people that want to take instead of give.** Jealous and mean-spirited people are intent on making themselves feel better by taking from others.

4.0 **Be as generous as possible in as many ways as possible.** Believe in the virtue that those who give will receive, and that helping others is both giving and receiving at the same time.

5.0 **Avoid giving based on conditions.** Be abundant; just give.

## Why Mesh Leaders Create a Better Workplace

 Being abundant in both thinking and doing is one of the big three of the Character Triangle. I want to be surrounded by people who think this way. I want to work and play with abundant "meshers."

What do Zipcar, Groupon, Netflix, Crushpad, and Thredup all have in common? They are new business models based on what Lisa Gansky describes in her brilliant new book *The Mesh: Why the Future of Business is Sharing*. A Mesh business is based on people coming together on a common platform to share in the use of goods or services. The commercial transaction is based on sharing. Gansky goes on to describe what she calls the "Virtuous Cycle of Trust": learn, test, engage, play...then rinse and repeat. I encourage you to read Gansky's book for the full meal deal description and understanding of Mesh. My point is that Mesh, at its foundation, is about abundant rather than scarcity thinking. It's all about expanding and sharing.

The virtuous cycle of trust is required between us as people in order to make sharing and partnering our preferred way of working. Hoarding resources is counterproductive. We need to leverage each other's skills rather than negatively minimize each other. As a CEO there is no way I have all the skills to run a company on my own. I need to mesh with all the people on my team so that we can leverage, expand and contract our capabilities as the environment around us changes. As a company we also need to partner more with other valuable members of our ecosystem. To borrow a phrase from Gansky, I guess we could call this Mesh Leadership.

I want to challenge us to think about how we can better

come together to share and leverage each other's skills. How can we abundantly give what we have developed in ourselves? How can we seek out and openly engage and receive what others have to offer? Where and how do we behave in fearful/scarce ways? How is that restrictive? Or even harmful? This is a different and a more complete thought than teamwork. It's bigger and more expansive. It is "Mesh."

I am at the early stages of more fully incorporating mesh thinking into abundance leadership. But I know it is important. Join me on the journey.

## Practice the Plays

Now that you've studied the Playbook, here is an opportunity to practice the plays themselves. Take the following actions and journal them below:

✔ Like the Nike commercial, JUST DO IT. Try being as sincerely generous as possible without expecting anything back in return. Don't be skeptical; instead, be open to the experience. Observe what happens. Don't quit when you feel like you're giving more than others. You probably are, so what?

_____

_____

_____

_____

_____

✔ Write down all the things you would like to see for yourself. Being able to write them down begins the process of expecting good things. However, focus on what you desire in the context of the value it provides to others or the cause it advances. This keeps the "I see myself winning a lottery" thoughts where they probably belong; in the mental wastebasket.

_____

_____

_____

_____

_____

➤ Observe people who are sincerely the most abundance-focused people you know. Watch what they do and say. What can you learn from these people? Which habits can you adopt to make yourself more abundant today?

_____

_____

_____

_____

_____

➤ Immediately begin to minimize time with people who are scarcity behaving people. Do it respectfully, but avoid these people. It's like quitting smoking; the damage begins to heal itself almost immediately. Begin to observe what changes in your life.

_____

_____

_____

_____

_____

✔ On the other hand, begin spending more time with abundance-focused people who see themselves as successful and always trying to make things better. By the way, they are likely high scorers on the self-accountability and respect scales as well.

_____

_____

_____

_____

_____

✔ Identify five ways you have acted in a more abundant way based on the principles of this chapter.

_____

_____

_____

_____

_____

# Personal Learning on Being Abundant

## Climbing to the Top of the Character Triangle

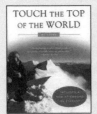 Erik Weihenmayer has climbed every major summit in the world. This is an incredible feat in its own right, but Erik makes this accomplishment astounding due to the fact that he is blind. You've probably all imagined the difficulty in climbing Mt. Everest... but climbing it blind? Erik has accomplished that. Now, that's character!

Erik embodies every element of the Character Triangle. When he became unexpectedly blind as a teenager, he could have blamed the world. Instead he asked himself "What?" and "How?" he might respond. How about deciding to climb every major challenge in the world? Now that is self-accountability.

Erik's life teaches us about respect by the way he prepares for every climb. He respects each peak and pays homage by the preparation and attention to detail. Additionally, he ropes up with every person on his team. He listens to each peak and the teams that help him reach it.

When it comes to being abundant, Erik also sets the bar. In Tibet, blindness is a basis for discrimination. When Erik became aware of this, he responded by embracing blind Tibetan kids and teaching them to climb...the pinnacle being Everest. Now, that's being abundant.

If you want to learn about someone who embodies the CT, read Erik's book *Touch the Top of the World* and check out one of his videos.[23]

---

[23] http://www.touchthetop.com/videos/ (Accessed March 2011)

I was on a trip to Japan with the executive colleagues of a Fortune 50 Company. It was a grueling three-week journey where we visited and intensely studied the best total quality and lean manufacturing companies. After two weeks of nonstop observation and analysis, we finally had a day to ourselves. I remember walking to the top of the mountain overlooking Kyoto, one of the great cultural cities of Japan. It was a holiday and as I climbed up the path I began noticing the small Buddhist shrines along the ascending trail.

At each shrine, I took a reflective moment to respectfully meditate. It took me about three hours to get to the top. I brought a journal with me and it was on the top of that hill where I wrote out what I wanted to accomplish in that organization. I literally visualized the possibilities and scenarios that would be great for the company—and for me.

After we returned from the trip, many of the things I visualized began to take place over the next few months. I was eventually promoted to report directly to the chairman of the company, and I became a catalyst in a journey that resulted in fundamental transformation of the organization. Of course, many other circumstances were involved to make that happen, but the point is *that what I visualized and wrote on that distant mountaintop really happened.*

It wasn't always this way. At times before and after this life-changing event, I allowed anxiety and scarcity to take over my thoughts, my actions and, in turn, my life. Rather than focusing on the possible, I became more concerned about the lack of something or another; I was focused on taking something away, rather than adding (Remember the LA Kings story in Chapter 1?).

In those cases, I tended to run away from, rather than drive to, what I really wanted and believed in. The more we embrace being abundant, the more we will take action.

# Free Yourself from "Prison" Now!

## Forgive that person and you can slam the cell door shut behind you for good.

 Forgiveness is an exercise of consciously freeing ourselves from resentment and anger. It is often difficult to begin the process of forgiveness, but the result is usually freeing and enormously gratifying. Do you and I have a process for engaging in real forgiveness?

Most of us feel that we have been hurt or wronged by someone. Often that person is in our workplace. After all, most of us spend most of our time in the work environment.

Do the following modified version of the 9-Step Exercise recommended by the Stanford Forgiveness Project[24]. Do it now. Here are the steps:

1. Make a list of all the people you feel have wronged you in some way; write down what each one did and why it's not okay.

2. Acknowledge that those things did happen, and that they did hurt you.

3. Make a commitment to yourself to do what you need to do in order to feel better.

4. Recognize that your distress is coming not from what happened, but from the thoughts that you have about what happened. Your thoughts are within your control.

5. When you feel yourself getting upset over what happened, practice stress reduction techniques to calm your body's fight or flight response.

---

[24] www.hawaiiforgivenessproject.org/Stanford.htm (Accessed March 2011)

6. Another thing you can try when you start getting upset about a past experience is to ask yourself, "What am I thankful for?" Ask this repeatedly until you feel better.

7. Put your energy into looking for ways to achieve your goals, instead of wasting your energy by continuously reliving the negative experiences in your mind.

8. Know that the best revenge against injustice is a life well lived. Forgiveness is about taking back your power.

9. Amend your grievance story to include how you moved on.

Marelisa Fabrega has a superb blog entitled *Abundance Blog at Marelisa online*. She recently posted a blog on forgiveness that is very comprehensive. I strongly urge you to read this entire blog. Much of this is a subset of her thorough work. She notes, and I really agree with her: "One of the things you and I should consider doing is forgiving those who have wronged us—whether we've experienced rejection, ridicule, deception, or abuse—and clearing out the mental clutter that comes from holding on to grudges and resentments. After all, the person that we hurt the most by holding on to resentment and anger is ourselves. Forgiving someone who has mistreated or wronged us is hard, isn't it? So, how do we forgive someone who has hurt us?"

Marelisa focuses on five ways to embark upon the journey of forgiveness in order to release ourselves from past hurts and rid ourselves of any emotional baggage which may be weighing us down and holding us back[25].

The areas include:

1. Rethink Your Definition of Forgiveness

---

[25] http://abundance-blog.marelisa-online.com/2010/12/15/how-to-forgive (Accessed March 2011)

2. If This Hadn't Happened, Would My Life Would Be Perfect?
3. What if You Don't Want to Forgive?
4. Questions to Ask Yourself to Help You Forgive
5. Nine-Step Forgiveness Exercise

I know of so many people at work (and of course in life outside of work) who have been dragging resentment and hostility towards one or more people. If I could give them a gift, it would be the act of forgiveness. Perhaps this blog, along with Marelisa's excellent work, and the resources she provides will provide an inspiration and process for doing so.

Start the process of forgiveness with at least one person now. Actively commit to it!

I started this book with a story about St. Nicholas, the junior high school in Edmonton where I worked for four years. I was young, full of energy and passion for the school. I played college football for the University of Alberta, had long hair down to my shoulders, and these kids naturally gravitated toward me.

At the time, I was a little insensitive and naïve about to how I made the more experienced and tenured teachers feel. One of these was a science teacher, in his fifties at that time. For this man, who was used to being the center of things, I think my bursting on the scene was a little too much. Rather than embracing my contributions in an abundant way to begin with, this guy took more of a scarcity approach. My contributions somehow became a personal loss for this guy.

One time at a staff party, I remember sitting on the stairs, putting on my shoes, wrapping up the evening. As this man was walking by me on the steps, he kicked me as hard as he could in my back. I think we were both stunned by his behavior. Frankly, I wanted to "straighten his tie"; but, thankfully, cooler heads prevailed. I believe my wife Kathleen, who observed this event, deftly navigated me away from the situation. In some small way I was reminded of how destructive scarcity behavior is. It generates fear and fear often leads us down an unhappy path, to failure, depression, and insecurity—even violence.

By the way, in the spirit of self-accountability, there are probably things I could have done, in retrospect, to help this man feel less of this scarcity toward me and the situation. However, after this experience, I became more vigilant and aware of the importance of attracting abundant-thinking people in my life.

We can't control the actions of others. However, we can control our own actions, and moving away from scarcity-thinking people is one sure way to attract more abundance in your life.

In the "life is weird" category, I want to share a mini-story within this one. Mark Messier, arguably one of the greatest hockey players on the history of the game, was eleven years old when I was a teacher at St. Nicholas. He was so full of enthusiasm; and when he came running into my gym class back then, he had that world-famous grin on his face!

You may recall earlier in the book that I became the VP of operations for the L.A. Kings Hockey Club. At that time, Mark was playing in New York for the Rangers. When the Kings traveled there, I joined them and made arrangements through our PR guy to say "Hello" to Mark. I wondered if he would even remember me, although I did teach at his dad's hockey school in the summer as well. Sure enough, after the game, Mark comes out of the dressing room and gives me a big hug, and says, "Mr. Rubis, how are you?"

"I need to be calling you, Mr. Messier, now," I responded.

We had a brief but nice reunion outside that dressing room. Would either of us have believed it, if on that gym stage in 1974 (the anecdote from Chapter 1), I had pointed at eleven-year-old Mark and said, "Hey, I'll see you in New York twenty years from now; you'll be one of greatest hockey players of the world and I'll be the VP of Operations for the LA Kings" Hmm!

By the way, speaking of self-accountability, Mark assured New York City and all Ranger fans that he would take personal leadership for winning the Stanley Cup and of course, in 1994, after a long drought, they did so. Messier was instrumental. At the same time, when you ask NHL players who they respect the most and who they would most want on their team, Mark's name is on the short list.

Mark Messier lives the Character Triangle when it comes to playing hockey.

---

*"People with a scarcity mentality tend to see everything in terms of win-lose. There is only so much; and if someone else has it, that means there will be less for me. The more principle-centered we become, the more we develop an abundance mentality, and the more we are genuinely happy for the successes, well-being, achievements, recognition, and good fortune of other people. We believe their success adds to...rather than detracts from... our lives."*
— Stephen R. Covey

---

## Two Cheetahs Could Lick You Today... Really!

 In the late nineties I was the COO of a publicly traded company and we took about 100 employees and their guests to a spa resort in San Diego as a "thank you" for great performance. As part of the trip, I had the privilege of hosting a beautiful dinner celebration at the San Diego Wild Animal Park. That evening Julie Scardina, the famous San Diego animal trainer and (at that time) regular guest on *The Tonight Show* with Jay Leno, brought a cast of her animals on stage to entertain and educate us all.

Prior to the trip I had a serious accident where I crushed my sternum and broke my collar bone along with a number of ribs. As I ambled on stage to wrap up the evening and to thank Julie, our CEO, and most importantly our team and guests, Julie unbeknown to me, released the two cheetahs she had with her (glad she kept hold of the boa constrictor). There I was bandaged up, in a sling, and these majestic cats gently joined me at center stage. They began licking my bruised arms and chest, a gesture of healing that will be with me forever. The crowd gasped and a surreal quiet came over the room.

I managed to keep my composure, looked at those beautiful creatures, and exclaimed into the microphone, "Who would have believed it if I would have told people at breakfast this morning that two cheetahs would be licking me up here on stage tonight?" That became the metaphor for the trip. No one can make up the wonders our life has in store for us.

Be open and take in the beauty of the unexpected. Accept.

# CHAPTER 5

# Character Triangle Points to Remember

## BE Accountable

**1.0 Improve yourself first.** Before asking or expecting from others, approach issues with self-examination of what and how you might contribute.

**2.0 Always ask what and how you might do something first.** Begin each interaction with yourself in control by taking responsibility for your action(s).

**3.0 Act self-accountable without expecting reciprocity.** Being accountable is more about your character than others'. You can be self-accountable regardless of what others do.

**4.0 Avoid blaming; especially self-blaming.** There is very little value, if any, in finding someone to blame.

**5.0 Watch out for the victim thinking often related to the word "they."** Waiting or wanting the often undefined or mysterious "they" to make things better is often frustrating for all.

## BE Respectful

**1.0 Be receptive and "look again."**

**2.0 Remember that everything is a process and all processes can be improved.** A process is distinct from the person.

**3.0 Always examine the process, behavior, and situation first; never attack a person.**

**4.0 Treat others the way you deserve to be treated.** Be nice.

**5.0 Listen with understanding; be present and look at every perspective.** Diverse angles and great dialogue is fundamental to being respectful.

**6.0 Use the STP process.** It is a great listening tool, problem-solving process, and a way to get people aligned.

## BE Abundant

**1.0 Being abundant is a state of mind.** If you see yourself as prosperous, you will be prosperous. If you see yourself as lacking, you will lack. Remember that you have to be self-abundant first.

**2.0 Take calculated risks.** Cherish the deeply held belief that things will work out for the best and that you have right to material wealth, peace of mind, and health.

**3.0 Avoid negative people and people that want to take instead of give.** Jealous and mean-spirited people are intent on making themselves feel better by taking from others.

**4.0 Be as generous as possible in as many ways as possible.** Believe in the virtue that those who give will receive. Avoid giving based on conditions. Be abundant; just give.

### Success is About Your Mindset! What's Yours?

 Okay...let's say you believe in Character Triangle values and are now "living in the Triangle"—that is, you have become a practitioner. You are taking real strides in being self-accountable and you are reflecting on what else might fuel your efforts. Think about this...what's your mindset?

At a recent sales conference one of our guest presenters reinforced the mindset that distinguishes successful salespeople. Carol Dweck, the Stanford psychologist, in her 2006 book Mindset outlines two primary categories of mindset: fixed and growth. Those of us with an orientation towards a fixed mindset see success as showing talent, while those of us with a growth mindset view success as a journey of development. Perhaps most revealing about the differences between those with a fixed vs. growth mindset is the reaction to adversity, self-assessment, and skill building. Essentially a growth mindset reinforces purposeful practice and the work put into the journey rather than the prize.

What mindset do you and I have? Part of the growth mindset is choosing to turn practice into a habit. The difference between thinking about practice then becomes different. It becomes who we *are,* not what we *do.*

Living with Character and applying the Character Triangle is **a belief and action habit system.** Each of the following is equally important to the CT's successful contribution in living out your life's purpose.

**Belief:** Don't just let this book be your "flavor of the month" idea before relegating it to your "business bookshelf" with all the other great ideas that sounded good in theory but never took root in your active, daily belief system. For the Character Triangle to have a personal impact, we must first understand it, and believe in its three core elements.

**Action:** Beliefs are the foundation, but they become alive when acted upon. As I began writing this book, my editor told me, "Lorne, don't just tell them what you mean; show them what to do." So when you truly begin to believe in the Character Triangle, you must take it one step further and act on those beliefs. Apply the playbook. Practice every day.

**Habit System:** We can't just live with Character when it's convenient. Living the Character Triangle must be a systematic and habitual part of your daily life plan. Additionally, the three values of Accountability, Respect, and Abundance act in reinforcing unison as a powerful trinity. Each value stands on its own legs but the CT is a habit system.

---

### How Will You Measure Your Life?
### The Character Triangle Will Help You Get There!

How will you measure your life? Clayton M. Christensen wrote an article with insight and impact addressed to his outgoing 2010 MBA class, and published in the July/August edition of the *Harvard Business Review* magazine[26].

The following are just a few Dr. Christensen's thought-provoking statements:

---

[26] http://hbr.org/2010/07/how-will-you-measure-your-life/ar/1 (Accessed March 2011)

"Doing deals does not yield the deep rewards that come from building up people."

Referring to the many students who return to their Harvard reunions years later unhappy, he said, "They didn't keep the purpose of their lives front and center as they decided how to spend their time, talents, and energy."

"People who are driven to excel have this unconscious propensity to under-invest in their families and over-invest in their careers...even though intimate and loving relationships with their families are the most powerful and enduring source of happiness."

"Culture, in compelling but unspoken ways, dictates the proven acceptable methods by which members of the group address recurrent problems, a powerful management tool."

"Like employees, children build self-esteem by doing things that are hard and learning what works."

"The marginal cost of doing something wrong "just this once" always seems alluringly low. It suckers you in, justification for infidelity and dishonesty, lies in the marginal cost economics of "just this once."

"It's easier to hold onto your principles 100 percent of the time than 98 percent of the time."

"It's crucial to take a sense of humility into the world. Generally you can be humble only if you feel good about yourself, and you want to help those around you feel good about themselves, too."

My favorite quote of all..."Don't worry about the level of individual prominence you have achieved; worry about the individuals you have helped become better people."

Being self-accountable means having a strategy for life, of which work/careers are only part of the story. We need a strategy and ways to measure success. Self-respect includes having the courage to be balanced. Abundance is being confident enough to know that managing your time, talent, and energy will turn out okay; you will have what you need.

If the Character Triangle helps one person, including myself, become a better person, then every moment I've spent thinking and writing about this has been worth it.

## Be Accountable, Be Respectful and Be Abundant: A Connected System

While each of the values specified in the Triangle **(Be Accountable, Be Respectful, Be Abundant)** are important in their own right, the most powerful application comes by connecting the values as a system every day in some way.

**Be Accountable:** When we are self-accountable, we are in control of what we choose to do. We rise or fall, good or bad, from our own decisions. We don't let blame, derail our good intentions, or allow finger-pointing to become a default setting at work. We drive the action and choose never to be the victim, regardless of the situation.

**Be Respectful:** By applying the value of respect, we are in such an active, patient, and alert listening mode that our choices and actions have the benefit of absorbing the unique angles and teachings resident in others. This makes every day an occasion for learning, sharing, and growing, which soon become habitual behaviors—to the benefit of one and all. Because we have been generous to others, they are sincerely willing to give us what we need. We give respect freely to all.

**Be Abundant:** These accountable and respectful habits are underscored by the power of thinking with abundance. We genuinely believe that the resources are there for us to make a material contribution, so we proceed with that view in mind. We are grateful for what we have and we create a picture in our minds of what we want to do. We can visualize our desired state and open ourselves up to the belief that the resources are there for us to get us where we need to go. Even if we are derailed by unforeseen circumstances or find difficult obstacles in our way, our attitude is such that we believe the resources will come when they are needed. We are also self-accountable for being resourceful.

## Everything is a Process—the Process is Everything

The Character Triangle is a powerful belief and action system for personally thriving and winning, but it is no quick fix. Instead, like nearly everything else of value, it is a process, a never-ending belief system that gets continuously tested, strengthened, shaken, adjusted, and buttressed by the day-to-day challenges of living and working in this turbulent world. We have to make it a habit system that is uniquely ours.

Every day provides us with many moments of truth where we must continually ask ourselves: Do we genuinely believe and actively live these values? We must answer truthfully if these moments are to reveal value and improvement opportunities for better living with character.

### Ordinary Man Lives Extraordinarily... Thanks, Dad

 My father, Leo Rubis, passed away on May 22, 2010. He wasn't big on speeches but spoke volumes to his family and friends by the way he lived. His legacy was that he gave us a road map for living with character—not perfection, of course.

He did so by connecting three powerful attributes in his daily life. He was one of the most self-accountable people I ever met. He never, as hard as life was, allowed himself to become a victim. He blamed no one for his status in life. When one job ended he got another.

When cancer hit, he put one foot in front of the other

and said thank you for the life he had. He defined respect by the way he treated everyone. To the day he died, he treated the nurses in the palliative care unit like they were the most important people on earth. But that was how he behaved everyday with everyone when he was well and the boss, too. He was known as a gentleman. He was also generous well beyond his means. Things were often tight financially but he never focused on the lack of anything; he just focused on giving the most valuable thing he had…himself. He was always there for his children, grandchildren, and others… driving somebody somewhere…slipping twenty dollars in someone's pocket. When he could have been resting, he was at one of the kids' games…cheering all on and expecting performance. He just gave.

My father combined self-accountability, respect, and abundance into something I now call the Character Triangle. I could easily rename it Leo's Triangle. The best thing is that his personification of these values demonstrated that an ordinary life, by Hollywood standards, could be extraordinary and accessible to all. I therefore elect my dad to the Character Hall of Fame—just an ordinary guy living in an extraordinary way.

Some days we will be more consistent than others. It is very difficult to avoid being washed over by the events of a moment and to feel like we might have regressed and possibly reacted outside of the Character Triangle. I have to remind myself daily and provide myself with ongoing areas for improvement. However, if we embrace these values and live them more often than not, if they truly do become habitual behaviors over time, then we will live with character.

## We Define Success

As a system, the Character Triangle helps us get the most out of our work (and life) situations. By applying **Accountability, Respect, and Abundance** together, that is, living in the Triangle, we put ourselves in much greater control. While we cannot control what others do, we can control how we think and act. We personally become the most important determinant for thriving and winning at work and life.

WARNING: Living in the Triangle does not equal perfection. For example, there may be factors outside of one's control that impact the outcome. Being cognizant of these enhances your decision-making. Applying the CT in tandem with one's own raw intelligence illuminates but does not guarantee the desired result. But when we live in the Triangle, we know the journey we've taken. We can be proud of that.

I have worked with thousands of people over the years and I have been able to observe those that have been most successful. In almost all cases these successful people score highly in each of the Character Triangle values.

Think about being evaluated by teammates, supervisors, and others over time. What if they had to stand up and briefly describe what they thought about you as a contributor? What would you want them to say about your work?…and life?

What if they said (write your name in all of the following blanks):

_____ is an excellent teammate and contributor!

_____ always takes personal responsibility, is a great listener, problem solver, and continually looks to make things better for all.

_____ provides great value to me and others.
_____ works with character, is an impact player,
and inspires people!
_____ is a winner and someone I would describe
as very successful in the most complete way.

## Connect Your Purpose to the Character Triangle

Over the years I have spent considerable time thinking about and working on my life's purpose. I once spent a week away on a personal excellence program, deep in the Oregon woods, on sort of a personal "anthropological dig" with the aim of better defining my life's purpose. My work on the Character Triangle had its genesis there. The essence of spending time on one's purpose is built around the belief that each of us will achieve a greater sense of fulfillment if we can define our life's mission and build on our core strengths and attributes. This goes beyond "form" (i.e. what type of job/career we have, e.g. engineer) or "outcome" (i.e. end result...e.g. make a lot of money). Developing a life's purpose is a deeper and more motivating concept. Ideally it is the basis for the action we take daily and in total summarizes our reason for being. My formal purpose statement has a spiritual, physical, and personal relationship dimension to it that I won't go into here. But my work purpose is to make a meaningful and lasting contribution by adding enormous value to others as a leader, teacher, and coach. I have been in many different roles and companies, but my personal work mission remains my anchor regardless of changing circumstances. In my current role I want to achieve all the success that is measured by financial means but this is not what drives me and gets me up in the morning.

I realize that many of us feel fortunate in a difficult

economic environment just to have a job. And all of us have a variety of personal ups and downs that can make the idea of a purpose statement seem almost trivial. It could even feel like an academic exercise to spend time on this. But my view is that investing in this is a very worthwhile and practical personal activity. Most of us don't have the luxury of going into the woods to self-reflect. But there is merit in having this intimate conversation with yourself over a cup of coffee or during a quiet walk. If you want a kick start, I suggest you get involved in an exercise called "What's Your Sentence."

I'm a fan of Dan Pink. Readers of his book, *Drive: The Surprising Truth about What Motivates Us*[27], may remember this exercise. It asks you to distill your life—what it's about, why you're here—into a single sentence. It's tough, but it's powerful. I encourage you to participate.

The Character Triangle is a value and habit system and when you apply it to your life's purpose it becomes exponential in its value to each of us and all the people we interact with. Please invest in yourself on this. Live the Character Triangle!

You're worth it.

---

[27] Daniel H. Pink, *Drive: The Surprising Truth About What Motivates Us*, Riverhead Books, New York, 2009, p. 154.

# Kindness*

*by*

*Naomi Shihab Nye*

Before you know what kindness really is
you must lose things,
feel the future dissolve in a moment
like salt in a weakened broth.
What you held in your hand,
what you counted and carefully saved,
all this must go so you know
how desolate the landscape can be
between the regions of kindness.
How you ride and ride
thinking the bus will never stop,
the passengers eating maize and chicken
will stare out the window forever.
Before you learn the tender gravity of kindness,
you must travel where the Indian in a white poncho
lies dead by the side of the road.
You must see how this could be you,
how he too was someone
who journeyed through the night with plans
and the simple breath that kept him alive.
Before you know kindness as the deepest thing inside,
you must know sorrow as the other deepest thing.
You must wake up with sorrow.
You must speak to it till your voice
catches the thread of all sorrows
and you see the size of the cloth.
Then it is only kindness that makes sense anymore,
only kindness that ties your shoes

and sends you out into the day to mail letters
and purchase bread,
only kindness that raises its head
from the crowd of the world to say
it is I you have been looking for,
and then goes with you everywhere
like a shadow or a friend.

*Reprinted by permission of the author. Naomi Shihab Nye, a Palestinian American freelance writer, editor, and speaker, is known for poetry, which lends a fresh perspective to ordinary events, people, and objects. She speaks out against terrorism and prejudice. In 2010 Naomi was elected a Chancellor of the Academy of American Poets. About her work, the poet William Stafford has said, "Her poems combine transcendent liveliness and sparkle along with warmth and human insight. She is a champion of the literature of encouragement and heart. Reading her work enhances life."*

# APPENDIX A:

# What and How

In the book *QBQ! The Question behind the Question, What to Really Ask Yourself to Eliminate Blame, Complaining, and Procrastination,*[28] author John G. Miller outlines the *What and How* process: "Now let's talk about the tool that brings personal accountability to life: the *QBQ*.

*The Question Behind the Question* is built on the observation that our first reactions are often negative, bringing to mind Incorrect Questions (IQs). But if in each moment of decision we can instead discipline our thoughts to look behind those initial questions and ask better ones (QBQs), the questions themselves will lead us to better results.

One of the guiding principles of the *QBQ* is, "The answers are in the questions," which speaks to the same truth: If we ask a better question, we get a better answer. So the *QBQ* is about asking better questions. But how can we tell a good question from a bad one? What does a "better" question sound like?

*QBQ* can help each of us learn to recognize and ask better questions. For starters, here are the three simple guidelines for creating a *QBQ*:

---

[28] G.P. Putnam's Sons, New York, 2004, p. 17–19,

1. **Begin with "What?" or "How?" (not "Why?" "When?" or "Who?").**

2. **Contain an "I" (not "they," "them," "we," or "you").**

3. **Focus on action.**

"What can I do?" for example, follows the guidelines perfectly. It begins with "What," contains an "I," and focuses on action: "What can I do?" Simple, as I said. But don't let its simplicity fool you. Like a jewel, the *QBQ* is made up of many facets.

# APPENDIX B:

## Situation–Target–Proposal

Over the years I have used a simple tool to help my listening dialogue: the STP Problem Solving Approach, Situation—Target—Proposal.[29] STP is timeless and yet so simple to apply:

### Situation (Define the Situation)

Generate and reach agreement on a comprehensive list of situation statements:

- What is the situation we are facing?

- What data do we have about what is going on?

- What is working well?

- What is wrong with the way things are going?

- Where is the problem occurring?

- How often, how much, and under what circumstances?

- How serious is this?

- What are people's reactions to what is going on?

---

[29] *Category Management Toolkit*. Office of Government Commerce. Office of HM Treasury: London, www.ogc.gov.uk, p.6–7.

- What might be the cause of the problem or situation?

- Ask the five W's and one H: Who? What? Where? When? Why? How?

- What might help or hinder identifying a feasible solution to the problem?

- Are there situational facts and data we do not have and need to collect?

## Target (Identify Targets)

Generate and reach agreement on a final list of target statements:

- How would you describe the ideal situation?

- What does success look like?

- What are our goals?

- How would things be different if the problem were solved?

- What differences would we like in the way we do things, in the way people work together, and in our methods or equipment?

- What major and minor outcomes do we want from this situation?

## Proposal (Develop Proposals)

Generate and reach agreement on a comprehensive list of proposal statements:

- How can we get from where we are to where we want to be?

- What can we do to solve the problem?

- What actions should we take to immediately remedy the situation?

- What actions should we take for long-term prevention?

- If we didn't have any constraints (time, financial, etc.) what could we do to solve the problem?

## Final Steps

Plan to close the S–T gap:

- Check for conflicting targets.

- Group S-statements that relate to the targets.

- Identify S–T gap.

- Identify proposals that close S–T gaps.

- Reach agreement on proposals to implement (may use ranking and voting to facilitate decision-making).

- Put proposals into action:

- Convert proposal into action.

- Plan—identify who does what and when.

Ensure the action plan assigns responsibilities to track completion and results.

# ACKNOWLEDGMENTS

I thank my sweetheart and wife Kathleen for her infinite patience and constant encouragement. She has always been the nudge behind the next step. Kathleen, thank you for the pages read, honest feedback, and belief in me. If I have done anything worthwhile in my life, you have been instrumental. Our children have been wonderful facilitators directly and indirectly. Our oldest, Keely, has used her marketing and PR prowess to guide much of my thinking in the presentation of this book. Her exceptional judgment is beyond her years. Our son Garrett has applied his journalism training to challenge and push every idea. His honest evaluations helped me find a voice. I could not have completed the book without his editing, unique angles, and fired-up perspective. Our daughter Jillian inspired my application of many elements resident in the Character Triangle, even as she launched a demanding career as a lawyer, while being the finest mother to our amazing grandson, Logan.

My sincere gratitude to Russell (Rusty) Fisher, who put a finer touch and perspective to my words. My executive assistant Lyn James is my constant supporter and the queen of competence and detail. She defines administrative excellence and has been a guide every step of the way. Her commitment to polishing my manuscript transformed it beyond words. Marly Cornell is an amazing editor. Her experience helped shape the final product and made it much more accessible. Alese Pickering is a world class designer. Her work on the Character Triangle logo is timeless and she knew exactly what the book cover should communicate. Nav Dael, my photographer, is a real pro and knows how to do more with less. And Langdon Street Press, my publisher, has a superb team lead by the exceptional author coordinators Danielle Adelman and Hannah Lee. The Character Triangle is the result of a high performing team. I will be eternally grateful to all of you.

I deeply thank the many friends, colleagues, and family members who patiently read through my manuscripts. I am so grateful that you shared your time and thoughts with kindness and consideration.

I must acknowledge the executives and team members at Ryzex and all my colleagues over the years. You have been the basis of everything I've learned about the Character Triangle. Thank you for allowing me to work by your side, and forgive me for times when I strayed from being self-accountable, respectful, and abundant. Finally, a special thanks to the "kids" of St. Nicholas. Your generosity has always been a source of strength and inspiration.

Loving you all in The Character Triangle,

Lorne

# ABOUT THE AUTHOR

Lorne Rubis is president and CEO of Ryzex, a global mobile technology solutions provider.

The constant in Lorne's diverse career is his ability to successfully lead organizations through significant change. At US WEST, where he served as a vice president/company officer, Lorne was one of only seven direct reports to the chairman, responsible for the strategic planning process, governance, and the company's worldwide total quality initiative.

After a brief but eventful stint at the LA Kings Hockey Club (where, as VP of Business Operations, he improved operations and oversaw the development of Staples Center's innovative premium seating strategy) he became VP of Sales and then chief operating officer at Multiple Zones (now Zones.com). There, he led the transformation of the company from a business-to-consumer enterprise to a business-to-business enterprise, realizing dramatic growth in revenue and e-Commerce. As CEO of Stellar One, he successfully took a privately held Internet protocol TV software company to market.

Lorne Rubis continues to be fully engaged in his role as president and CEO of Ryzex while actively expanding his interest as an author on matters related to leadership, culture, and character.

Lorne and his wife Kathleen split their time between their homes in Bellingham and Mercer Island, Washington.

# BIBLIOGRAPHY and REFERENCES

## Books

Ariely, Dan. *The Upside of Irrationality: The Unexpected Benefits of Defying Logic at Work and at Home*, Harper, New York, 2010.

Bogle, John. *Enough: True Measures of Money, Business, and Life*, John Wiley & Sons, Hoboken, NJ, 2009.

Charan, Ram. *Know-How: The 8 Skills that Separate People Who Perform from Those Who Don't*, Crown Business, New York, 2007.

Collins, James C. and Jerry I. Porras. *Built to Last: Successful Habits of Visionary Companies*, Harper Business, New York, 1994.

Csikszentmihalyi, Mihaly. *Finding Flow: The Psychology of Engagement with Everyday Life*, Basic Books, New York, 1997.

Davis, Dr. Richard. *The Intangibles of Leadership*, Jossey-Bass, Mississauga, ON, 2010.

Dweck, Carol. *Mindset*, Ballantine Books, New York, 2008.

Friedman, Thomas L. *The World is Flat: A Brief History of the Twenty-First Century*, Farrar, Straus and Giroux, New York, 2007.

Gansky, Lisa. *Mesh: Why the Future of Business is Sharing,* Portfolio Penguin, New York, 2010.

Godin, Seth. *Linchpin: Are You Indispensible?* Portfolio (Penguin), New York, 2010.

_____*Permission Marketing: Turning Strangers into Friends, and Friends into Customers,* Simon & Schuster, New York, 1999.

Hill, Linda A. and Kent Lineback. *Being the Boss: The Three Imperatives for Becoming a Great Leader,* Harvard Business Review Press, Boston, 2011.

Imai, Massaaki. *Kaizen: The Key to Japan's Competitive Success,* McGraw-Hill, New York, 1986.

Lazare, Dr. Aaron. *On Apology,* Oxford University Press, 2004.

Miller, John. *QBQ! The Question Behind the Question,* G. P. Putnam & Sons, New York, 2004.

Patterson, Kerry, Joseph Grenny, Ron McMillan, and Al Switzler. *Crucial Conversations: Tools for Talking when the Stakes are High* McGraw-Hill, New York, 2002.

Peters, Tom. *The Little Big Things: 163 Ways to Pursue Excellence,* Harper Studio, New York, 2010.

_____*Thriving on Chaos: Handbook for a Management Revolution,* Harper & Row, New York, 1987.

Phillips, Adam, and Barbara Taylor. *On Kindness,* Farrar, Straus and Giroux, New York, 2009.

Pink, Daniel H. *A Whole New Mind: Moving from the Information Age to the Conceptual Age,* Riverhead Books, New York, 2005.

_____*Drive: The Surprising Truth About What Motivates Us*, Riverhead Books, New York, 2009.

Rao, PhD, Srikumar S. *Are You Ready to Succeed, Unconventional Strategies for Achieving Personal Mastery in Business and Life*, Hyperion, New York, 2006.

Rifkin, Jeremy. *The Empathic Civilization: The Race to Global Consciousness in a World in Crisis*, J.P. Tarcher/Penguin, New York, 2009.

Schawbel, Dan. *Me 2.0*, Kaplan Publishing, New York, 2009.

Senge, Peter. *The Fifth Discipline: The Art and Practice of the Learning Organization*, Doubleday/Currency, 1990.

Singer, Peter. *The Life You Can Save*, Random House, New York, 2009.

Tolle, Eckhart. *A New Earth, Awakening to Your Life's Purpose*, Dutton/Penguin Group, New York, 2005.

Weihenmayer, Erik. *Touch the Top of the World: A Blind Man's Journey to climb Farther than the Eye can See*, Plume, New York, 2002.

Wooden, John and Don Yaeger. *A Game Plan for Life: John Wooden's Lessons on Mentoring*, Bloomsbury USA, New York, 2009.

## Online Resources

Abundance: http://abundance-blog.marelisa-online.com/

Category Management Toolkit: www.ogc.gov.uk

Curphy-Roellig Followership Model: http://www.
co2partners.com/blog/2010/06/followership/

Forgiveness: http://www.hawaiiforgivenessproject.org/
Stanford.htm

Ideas Worth Spreading: http://www.ted.com/

Mind Mapping: http://en.wikipedia.org/wiki/Mind_map

Organizational Performance: http://www.vitalsmarts.com/

Project Management: http://www.businessballs.com/
project.htm

Seven Management and Planning Tools: http://
en.wikipedia.org/wiki/Seven_Management_and_
Planning_Tools

Spiritual Intelligence:  http://www.deepchange.com/

## Individual Websites

| | |
|---|---|
| Abbott, Jim | www.jimabbott.net |
| Ariely, Dan | www. danariely.com |
| Bogle, John | www. johncbogle.com / wordpress |
| Bauata, Leo | www.zenhabits.com |
| Charan, Ram | www.ram-charan.com |
| Chua, Celestine | www. celestinechua.com |
| Davis, Dr. Richard A. | www. intangiblesofleadership.com |
| Dinsmore, Scott | www.readingforyoursuccess.com |
| Dweck, Carol | www. mindsetonline.com |
| Ehrenreich, Barbara | www.barbaraehrenreich.com |
| Fabrega, Marelisa | www. abundance-blog.marelisa-online.com |
| Ferriss, Tim | www.fourhourworkweek.com / blog |
| Friedman, Thomas L. | www.thomaslfriedman.com |
| Gansky, Lisa | www. lisagansky.com |
| Glennie, Dame Evelyn | www.evelyn.co.uk |
| Godin, Seth | www.sethgodin.com / sg |
| Hill, Linda A. and Kent Lineback | www.beingtheboss.com |
| Miller, John | www.qbq.com |
| Peters, Tom | www.tompeters.com |
| Pink, Dan | www.danpink.com |
| Rao, Srikumar S., PhD | www.areyoureadytosucceed.com |

| | |
|---|---|
| Rubis, Lorne | www.lornerubis.com |
| Schawbel, Dan | www.danschawbel.com |
| Singer, Peter | www.thelifeyoucansave.com |
| Tolle, Eckhart | www.eckharttolle.com/home |
| Weihenmayer, Erik | www.touchthetop.com |
| Wigglesworth, Cindy | www.deepchange.com |

# INDEX

## A

Abbott, Jim, 92

abundance, 85–117

as part of Character Triangle, 6, 125–126

"artists," 88

attitude, 89–93

forgiveness, 112–114

generosity, 86, 98

mesh leaders, 105–106

optimism, 94

perseverance, 92

personal learning, 110–116

playbook, 104

points to remember, 120

positive reinforcement, 98, 103

practice, 107–109

sharing, 105–106

as a state of mind, 93–99

visualization, 111

accountability, 13–48

as part of Character Triangle, 6, 125

apologizing, 44–45

bad experiences, labeling, 18

blame, 19–20, 22–25, 26–27

bosses, 41–42, 43

complaining, 32–33

crises, 24

feedback in the workplace, 37

forgiveness, 47

key steps, 26–28

personal control, 30–35

playbook, 36

points to remember, 119

positive resilience, 18

practice, 38–40

self-blame, 26–27

taking personal action, 20–22

understanding of, 17

victimization, 19

action habit system, 121–122

adversity, 18, 92, 121

Angelou, Maya, 84

Anschutz, Phil, 42, 84

apologizing, 44–46

arrogance, 55–56, 82–83

artists, 88

assessment, 121

attacking the process, 34–35, 79, 82–83

attitudes, 60, 89–93

avoidance, 26–27

**B**

Babuata, Leo, 83

bad experiences, labeling, 18

being present, 57, 67–68, 79, 83

*Being the Boss,* 41

belief and action habit system, 121–122, 126

Belkin, Lisa, 44–46

blame, 6, 19–20, 22–25, 26–27

blog, author's (www.lornerubis.com), 11

bosses, 41–42, 43

Bregman, Peter, 59–60

Browne, Rud, xvii-xviii

bullying, 51

**C**

capitalism, 66

career advice, 14

challenges, xv, xvii, 21, 32, 42, 126

character, defining, 5

Character Triangle (CT)

a connected system, 125–126

described, 5–7

life purpose connection, 129–130

origin of, 3

points to remember, 119–120

the process is everything, 126–127

cheetahs, 117

children, 123

Christensen, Clayton M., 122–123

climbing, 110

communication

crucial conversations, 71–72

listening, 51–53, 57, 60, 61–63, 68

miscommunication, 59–60

complaining, 30, 32–33

condescending behavior, 55–56, 82–83

confidence, 15, 25, 34

courage, 24, 25, 47, 124

Covey, Stephen, 116

CRIB concept, 71

crises, 24

crucial conversations, 71–72

*Crucial Conversations,* 71

culture, 51, 74-75, 123

Czlonka, Henry, 1–2

**D**

dad, 81, 86, 126-127

diversity, 63–64, 74

*Drive: The Surprising Truth about What Motivates Us,* 37, 130

Dunn, Elizabeth, 98

Dweck, Carol, 121

**E**

Ehrenreich, Barbara, 94

email, 61

*The Empathic Civilization,* 54

empathy, 54

encouragement, 98, 103

everything is a process, 58–61, 79, 126–127

excellence, 65, 98, 103, 129

**F**

Fabrega, Marelisa, 113

family, 123

feedback in the workplace, 37

forgiveness, 47, 112–114

Friedman, Thomas L., 20

**G**

Gansky, Lisa, 105

generosity, 7, 66, 81, 86, 88, 92, 97–99, 107, 125–127

giving, 7, 37, 58, 97, 98, 104

Glennie, Evelyn, 57

Godin, Seth, 88

Grenny, Joseph, 71

Gulf oil crisis, 20, 24, 45

**H**

habit system, 121–122

Harvard Business Review, 59, 122

Hayward, Tony, 45

Heath, Dan, 101

Hill, Linda A., 41

honesty, 34

how and what questions, 21, 46, 48, 90, 135–136

Hreljac, Ryan, 25

humility, 123

**I**

Ivy League, 55-56

**K**

Kafka, Franz, 68

Kagan, Elena, 55–56

kindness, 65–67, 83, 132–133

*Kindness,* 132–133

knowing coworkers, 50

**L**

lack/lacking, xviii, 31, 90, 92-93, 99, 101, 104, 111,120, 127

law of attraction, 95

Lazare, Aaron, 44

leadership, xv-xvi, 24, 32-33, 42, 65

learning, personal, 41, 79, 110

Lieweke, Tim, 42–44

*The Life You Can Save,* 101

life's purpose, 14, 122–123, 129–130

Lillis, Chuck, xv, 87–89

linchpins, 88

*Linchpins, Supporters and Leeches,* 88

Lineback, Kent, 41

listening, 51–53, 57, 60, 61–63, 68

with understanding, 6, 55, 59, 61, 73, 120

*The Little Big Things,* 65, 98

Los Angeles Kings Hockey Club, 42–44, 84, 115–116

**M**

McCormick, Dick, 82, 86

McDonald, Kirby, 84

McMillan, Ron, 71

measuring your life, 122–123

*The Mesh,* 105

mesh leadership, 105–106

Messier, Mark, 115

Miller, John, 19, 21, 135–136

mind, stillness of, 68

mindset, 121

miscommunication, 59–60

morale, 81

Mother Teresa, 50

**N**

*A New Earth, Awakening to Your Life's Purpose,* 92–93

Nye, Naomi Shihab, 132–133

**O**

*On Kindness,* 66

optimism, 94

**P**

Patterson, Kerry, 71

performance reviews, 37

perseverance, 92

personal attacks, 34–35, 51–52, 58–59, 79, 82–83

personal control, 30–35

Peters, Tom, 44, 52, 65, 98

Phillips, Adam, 66

pinging the universe, 14

Pink, Dan, 37, 130

Plato, 65

playbook, 36, 76, 104

positive reinforcement, 98, 103

positive resilience, 18

*Power Talk,* 91

powerlessness, xvii, 41

practice (the plays), 38, 76, 107

presence, 68, 83

process, 58, 61-62, 73, 79, 120, 126-127

purpose

    life's, 121, 129

    statement, 129–130

**Q**

*QBQ! The Question Behind the Question,* 135–136

questions to ask, 21, 46, 48, 90, 135–136

**R**

Rao, Srikumar S., 18

recognition at work, 37, 81, 98, 123

relationships, 6, 59, 123

reputation, 55, 80

respect, 49–84

    as part of Character Triangle, 6, 125

being present, 67–68

condescending behavior, 55–56, 82–83

crucial conversations, 71–72

defined, 53, 55

diversity, 63–64

empathy, 54

everything is a process, 58–61, 79

getting to know people, 50

kindness, 65–67, 83

listening, 51–53, 57, 60, 61–63, 68

miscommunication, 59–60

morale, 81

personal learning, 79–80

playbook, 73

points to remember, 120

practice, 76–78

recognition by peers, 81

self-respect, 53–56

Situation - Target - Proposal (STP), 62–63

status of individuals, 55–56, 82–83

teamwork, 70

unconditional, 57–58

world views, 74

responsibility, assuming. *See* accountability

Rifkin, Jeremy, 54

Robbennolt, Jennifer, 45

Robbins, Anthony, 91

Roski, Ed, 42, 84

Rubis, Leo, 126–127

Ryzex, 50–53

**S**

St. Nicholas School, 1–4, 79, 114–116, 142

scarcity, 89

Scardina, Julie, 117

self-accountability. *See* accountability

self-blame, 27

self-doubt, 96

self-esteem, 123

self-respect, 53–56

sharing, 105–106

Singer, Peter, 101

Situation - Target - Proposal (STP), 62–63, 137–139

smiling, 66, 94, 103

social media, 61

spiritual intelligence, 74–75

Stafford, William, 133

Stanford Forgiveness Project, 112–113

status of individuals, 55–56, 82–83

stillness of the mind, 68

strategy for life, 124

success, defining, 9–10, 31, 128–129

Switzler, Al, 71

**T**

Taylor, Barbara, 66

teamwork, 70, 90

Thomas, Ed, 47

Tolle, Eckhart, 92–93

trust, 55, 89, 105–106

Tucson mass shooting, 74

**U**

US WEST, 82–83, 86–89

**V**

victimization, 19

"Virtuous Cycle of Trust," 105

visualization, 111

**W**

website, author's
(www.lornerubis.com), 11, 63

websites, 149

Weihenmayer, Erik, 110

what and how questions, 21, 46, 48,
90, 135–136

"What's Your Sentence," 130

Wooden, John, 91

work environment, 60, 105–106

world views, 74

Wrigglesworth, Cindy, 74–75

**Z**

Zones, Inc., 46, 93–95